D0984527

Management,
Governance
and Leadership

A GUIDE FOR
COLLEGE AND UNIVERSITY
ADMINISTRATORS

Management, Governance and Leadership

JOHN D. MILLETT

A DIVISION OF AMERICAN MANAGEMENT ASSOCIATIONS

Library of Congress Cataloging in Publication Data

Millett, John David, 1912–
    Management, Governance and Leadership

    Includes index.
    1. College administrators—United States. I. Title.
LB2341.M4629   378′.111′0973   80-12930
ISBN 0-8144-5644-8

First Printing

Preface

I have written this book as a guide for leaders and managers in higher education. For the most part the ideas set forth herein express thoughts and concerns which I have been writing about for nearly 30 years. My first book about higher education was published in 1952, at the conclusion of a three-year study sponsored by the Association of American Universities. In the intervening years it has been my privilege to have served as president of Miami University in Ohio, as the first chancellor of the Ohio Board of Regents, and as a vice-president of the Academy for Educational Development, in association with my long-time friend, Alvin C. Eurich. Throughout these years—19 in Ohio and eight with the Academy—I have had the opportunity to write extensively about the organization, management, planning, and financing of colleges and universities.

In this work I have tried to bring together my basic thinking on the subject of organization and management of a university. It was inevitable that I should also say something about planning and financing. The focus here is primarily upon the university as an organization, but we cannot consider organization apart from purpose. If proper attention is to be given to management of the university, we cannot avoid concern with planning and financing. The problem in any discussion such as this one is to find limits to what one wants to say.

This book is not a synthesis of research, a report on original discovery, or an autobiography of personal experience. To be sure, my reading, my experience, and my thinking have influenced what I have said. I would like to think of the book as a distillation of ideas gathered from many sources, including consultation with college and university administrators.

I employ the word "university" here in a generic sense to refer to the more than 3,000 campuses of colleges, universities, schools, and institutes which comprise the universe of higher education in the United States. At times I have used the more cumbersome phrase "colleges and universities," and, although I had expected to avoid the phrase "institutions of higher education" throughout, I find that I have not always done so—in spite of good intentions. University and higher education are synonymous in this book.

I have endeavored to direct attention to the campus; not to multi-campus systems, not to state boards of higher education, not to agencies of the federal government, not to the general purpose foundations that do so much for higher education, not to the many associations of colleges and universities and of their staffs, which advance both intellectual performance and campus well-being. In the world of higher education, the campus is where the action is, where learning in its many modes takes place, where students gather, where faculty members respond to their high calling.

I believe one never fully recovers from the experience of being a student or from the challenge of being a professor. I do not pretend that I was a reluctant administrator. But as an administrator and as a consultant I have never had any illusions about the administrative role. The administrator is indispensable to academic performance and achievement. I spent 19 years, off and on, at a great university that lacked a president through all those years. I know from experience that faculty members can manage learning. I know from experience that faculty members cannot manage a university as an enterprise, as a learning environment. The administrator in a university leads an enterprise; he or she does not and cannot lead learning. I have tried here to present the reality of the university as an enterprise, as a place where people come together to learn, and to make learning possible. The faculty member is the epitome of scholarship and creative talent. The student is the aspiring learner. The administrator and his entourage of associates seek to encourage faculty members to develop their scholarship and students to develop their intellectual and skilled competencies, while asking society to support both faculty and students—and to leave both alone. I never found it useful or helpful to draw invidious distinctions between faculty members, students, staff, alumni, and political friends (or even enemies). Higher education is many kinds of people working together. Learning is more than faculty members practicing their craft or students sharpening their wits. Learning as undertaken in a university is an organized enterprise, and it is that enterprise as an organization which I have sought to outline with its unique attributes.

I wish to emphasize that the tabular and chart materials at the beginning of each chapter have special importance. These tables and charts serve a dual purpose: (1) to outline the basic concepts I will present, and (2) to set forth the comprehensive scope of the ideas summarized in the discussion. Indeed, the discussion in some chapters is less comprehensive than the tabular outline. If I had undertaken to discuss every entry in these outlines, this volume would have become much more lengthy than was my intention.

The tables and charts stand by themselves. The discussion illustrates my ideas without endeavoring to develop the details of each proposition. The tables and charts are comprehensive; the discussion is selective and suggestive. I hope every reader will give particular and careful attention to the tables and charts.

The reader will find overlappings of thought and expression in various places. This lends emphasis to observations and comments of great importance to me, and such emphasis was indeed a major objective in the writing of this volume.

Years ago, a college president said to me that he had learned that a little college could be a dangerous thing. I have learned that only a little thought about the university as an enterprise can be a dangerous thing. I hope no one will confuse my effort to be brief with a lack of thought. Perhaps the thought expressed briefly will still convey my profound admiration for the American university and all the persons associated with it, and my pride in having been a small part of this great endeavor in the years since I entered college as a timorous freshman in 1929.

I am indebted to Barbara Conway for assistance in preparing the manuscript.

John D. Millett

Author's Note

ON FACULTY COLLECTIVE BARGAINING

The observations presented in this book presume a faculty structure fully integrated in the management and governance processes of the university. In my judgment, the thrust to faculty collective bargaining cannot fail but to disrupt both the structure and the process of faculty management and governance. The full extent of such disruption is still to be assessed, but various studies (for example, that of Kemerer and Baldridge*) clearly indicate that faculty collective bargaining does have a major impact upon the faculty role and status in a university.

Because it has been influenced by the industrial model—a model that I reject both as a description of and as a prescription for university organization—faculty collective bargaining must necessarily draw a distinction between faculty and management. And once that distinction is drawn, the relationship becomes not one of collegial collaboration but rather one of adversary conflict. The result can only be a decline or substantial modification of the faculty role in university management.

To be sure, as a result of the Yeshiva University case in 1980 the faculty may come to be defined in private colleges and universities as a part of management. The national labor relations law will then no longer be applicable. Within the scope of state government labor relations laws, faculty members will have to be defined as public employees in order to engage in collective bargaining, and one wonders what effects that status will have on the management role of faculty members. It is possible to envisage a development whereby

* Frank R. Kemerer and J. Victor Baldridge, *Unions on Campus* (San Francisco: Jossey-Bass Publishers, 1975).

faculty members will find most if not all of their management duties assumed by deans and their staffs.

When the management role of faculty members is eroded, there must inevitably be some erosion in the governance authority of faculty members. For example, I can imagine a time when desirable degree programs and degree program course requirements will be determined by deans rather than by a faculty body or a faculty senate. Indeed, it appears to me that a collective bargaining agreement not only supersedes any bylaws or ordinances of faculty governance, but also limits faculty participation in campus governance. If I were an administrative officer today under circumstances of a faculty collective bargaining agreement, I would be very cautious about involving faculty members in decisions on matters not specified in the agreement.

Let me make my position clear. I see faculty collective bargaining not as a threat to academic administrators, but as a threat to faculty status. I know that many faculty members today feel that their status has already been substantially altered by state boards of higher education, by multi-campus systems of governance, by state government administrators and chief executives, and by state law. And some faculty members, observing collective bargaining by other groups of public employees, fear that a failure to take advantage of state labor relations laws may somehow be a mistake. I sympathize with these concerns, but I believe that there are means for coping with them that are better suited to the unique character of the university than faculty collective bargaining is.

If I were an administrative officer of a university today, I would welcome faculty collective bargaining as a new device calculated to strengthen and enhance administrative power. But I would see its advent as destructive to the collegial relationships that I hold to be desirable within the academic community and the academic enterprise.

John D. Millett

Contents

Management, Governance and Leadership

THE MEANING OF ORGANIZATION

Organizational Pluralism	Kinds of Organizations	Characteristics of Organizations	Units of Organization
Family	Family Units	Sense of Purpose	Output Units
Economy	Business Units	Work Specialization	Support Units
Services	Corporations	Work Technology	Governance Units
Religious	Proprietors	Pattern of Cooperation	Leadership Units
Denominations	Partnerships	Pattern of Management	
Educational	Non-Profit	Pattern of Governance	
Agencies	Health	Pattern of Leadership	
Associations	Other		
Polity	Religious Bodies		
	Parishes		
	Churches		
	Education		
	Schools		
	Colleges		
	Universities		
	Associations		
	Labor		
	Professions		
	Community		
	Voluntary		
	Organizational		
	Government-I		
	Federal		
	State		
	Local		
	Government-II		
	Legislative		
	Executive		
	Judicial		
	Bureaucracy		

1

The Meaning of Organization

Organization is a structure of relationships among people joined together for a common purpose at a particular time and in a particular place. In this broad sense, the term organization may be applied to a considerable variety of social arrangements, from the family to the polity or political system, from voluntary associations to religious bodies. It is our intention in this discussion, however, to focus on a general type of organizational structure, the productive enterprise, and more particularly to focus on a certain kind of productive enterprise, the university.

It may be argued that all social relationships involve some set of productive goals, that all organizations of people come together to produce some kind of goods and services. In a large sense, this claim may be factually accurate. It may be said that families produce a sense of security, that religious bodies promote a sense of spiritual well-being, that government organs of decision making provide an essential sense of social need, that voluntary associations of individuals develop a sense of common interest. I would argue, however, that these achievements, important as they are, do not fit our usual economic definition of goods and services, and should not be confused with organizational structures more specifically concerned with productive output.

By productive enterprises I have in mind business corporations and business firms of all kinds, farms, government agencies (the bureaucracy, if you please), military forces, hospitals, professional practitioners, museums and art galleries, commercial and nonprofit organizations of the performing arts, and schools and universities engaged in turning out the goods and services necessary to our material and mental well-being, including food, shelter, clothing, national security, health, buildings, aesthetic enjoyment, and intellectual development. I would emphasize that the university is a productive enterprise engaged in satisfying basic needs of people in society in much the same way that other, more familiar kinds of enterprise are.

At the same time, for various reasons to be advanced in the course of this discussion, I would emphasize that the university is a unique kind of productive enterprise, different in purpose, process, and structure from any of these other enterprises. The university stands in contrast with these other enterprises; comparisons must be made with caution and even with considerable skepticism. I do not agree with the proposition that universities share many common characteristics with business enterprises, with government administrative agencies, with the armed forces, or with the performing arts.

Before I undertake to consider the unique characteristics of the university, it may be useful to look in general at the common characteristics or attributes that scholars and observers identify in the organizational arrangements of productive enterprises. It must be understood that sociologists, political scientists, and business organizational theorists seldom use the same words or the same concepts in describing and prescribing organizational structures. Apart from the concept of bureaucracy—a concept subject to varied formulation—only a few other phrases are commonly employed in these discussions of organizational arrangements. One may frequently encounter such words or phrases as hierarchy, functional specialization, chain of command, span of control, and line and staff, but one cannot be certain that the meanings are the same when used by different commentators.

I shall review in my own words the common characteristics of organizational structure as I have gleaned them from over 45 years of reading and discussion. The words and phrases are my own; the ideas are those of many individuals who have written about their experience and their observation of organizations. And my own experience and observation have had their impact upon the discussion.

It is necessary to remind ourselves at the outset that the structure of relationships we are describing are relationships among people; they are social relationships in the setting of a productive enterprise. The term organization may on occasion be employed to refer to biological relationships, such as the structure of the human anatomy or of other living organisms; it may on occasion be employed to refer to physical relationships, such as the structure of matter or the structure of the solar system. These structural relationships are important, of course, but they are different in fundamental ways from the relationship of people joined together in a productive enterprise.

In addition, it is necessary to remind ourselves of the difference between a generalized description of a social organization and a particular social unit. When we speak of business firms, of government agencies, of hospitals, and of universities we are indulging in the convenience of an intellectual construct. Such groupings of units of similar purpose and process into a generalized kind or a universal type are essential to human discourse and to human intelligence. We need to bear in mind, however, that these groupings have no reality other than that of conceptualization. The reality of public sensory perception is the reality of a particular enterprise: the reality of a particular business corporation such as General Motors Corporation; of a particular government agency such as the Department of State in the federal government; of a particular hospital such as Bellevue Hospital in New York City; or of a particular university such as Harvard University or the University of Michigan.

The reality of the society of which we are all a part is the reality of an individual family, of an individual business firm, of an individual religious denomination and church, of an individual school, of an individual association, of an individual university. We identify common characteristics among these thousands and millions of units, and we classify these common characteristics into various groupings and sub-groupings in order to advance our understanding of the complex society in which we participate. We must never forget, however, that the generalizations we need for the convenience of intellectual discourse are abstractions, and that the reality of our social endeavor lies in the particular enterprise where our actual experience occurs.

Throughout this discussion we shall from necessity be considering "the university" as if there were in fact some readily identifiable entity of common existence which we might observe and analyze in terms of its structural relationships. In truth, of course, there is no such entity as "the university." Instead, there are some 3,000 campuses throughout the United States which comprise the universe of "the university" in our society. And each one of these 3,000 campuses is different from any other: different in location, different in program, different in size of enrollment, different in sponsorship, different in financial and other resources, different in the persons who comprise the enterprise. The generalizations we set forth here are only generalizations. In any given situation on any given campus the reality may be different. We can do no more here than to suggest concerns and circumstances which may have some general applicability, and which must then be adapted to the needs of a particular campus and of particular people.

SOME COMMON CHARACTERISTICS OF ORGANIZATION

Sociologists and social psychologists have often observed that American society is a society of organizations. They point out that our productive endeavors (our output of goods and services) are undertaken primarily through fairly sizable aggregations of persons. Most individuals in our society participate in one or more productive enterprises which bring together a considerable number of people who, working together, produce the goods and services we consume. Very few individuals, and very few family units, produce all the goods and services we need and want. The productive effort of America is essentially the productive effort of organizations.

Because we are a society of organizations, scholars in the behavioral sciences and in applied behavioral sciences have sought to identify and describe certain common characteristics of organizational relationships in productive enterprises. The words and phrases of these descriptions are often different, but the concepts are usually similar.

For my own understanding of the immense literature about organization I have found it useful to identify the following seven common characteristics of productive enterprise:

1. Sense of purpose.
2. Specialization of work effort.

3. Work technology.
4. Pattern of cooperation.
5. Pattern of management.
6. Pattern of governance.
7. Pattern of leadership.

Before I turn to some elaboration of these characteristics, I need to say something about the interaction of organizations with an external environment. Some writers are disposed to insist that organizations are continually adjusting to their environment, and to a certain extent the contention is undoubtedly correct. No enterprise can be indifferent to, or remain unaffected by, its economic, political, and social environment. The economic environment may encourage expansion or contraction of output, may encourage investment in plant or disinvestment, may encourage price stability or price instability. The political environment may encourage increased concern with occupational health and safety, increased concern with product standards, increased concern with collective bargaining, and increased concern with plant location. The social environment may encourage increased concern with patterns of employment, with community services, with training and educational opportunities, with demographic trends, and with community leadership.

Organizational structures do respond to environmental factors. If output is expanding, organizational structure is necessarily adjusted to fit the needs of larger scale. If output is constrained by the need to reduce pollution of water and air, organizational structure is necessarily adjusted to fit new standards of production technology. If output is dependent upon an available supply of technical and professional personnel, then organizational structure is necessarily adjusted to accommodate the numbers of persons who can be provided by the community or imported into the community.

These economic, political, and social factors in the external environment of a productive enterprise are of major importance. Moreover, these environmental influences may change over time, they may be different in their impact at one time in contrast with another time. Exactly how organizational structures respond to their environment is not entirely certain, but that they do respond is unquestionable. The most obvious response is a contraction or expansion in the size of the operation, in the volume of output, and in the magnitude of employment. Other responses may be more subtle and may take longer to effect.

Although I shall be referring to these environmental impacts upon organizational structure only in passing, I would emphasize that no organization can remain untouched by environmental concerns. Adjustments do take place in organizational structure because of economic, political, and social changes. None of the observations to be set forth in this discussion are intended to ignore or to underestimate the impact of external circumstance upon internal relationships of people within an organization.

SENSE OF PURPOSE. A major common characteristic of organizational structure is a defined sense of purpose. Productive enterprises are not created, continued, and modified because they are inherently desirable. They exist, survive, and adapt because they serve some useful purpose, because they provide needed and wanted outputs. People join an organization not solely because they want a job and income but also because they wish to have a part in producing useful goods and useful services.

Obviously, purposes may be of different scope and of different intensity. Some organizations may have a single purpose, such as selling jewelry or baking bread and pastries. Some organizations may have many purposes, related or unrelated, such as a retail department store and a producer of energy from diverse sources (coal, oil, natural gas, water, nuclear, and solar). Some organizations insist upon the indispensable utility of their goods or services. Some organizations appear to be almost indifferent about whether or not their goods and services are utilized.

Organizations define their purposes with varying degrees of precision. Some organizations devote considerable attention, time, and effort to the definition of their purpose or purposes, communicate these purposes extensively, and review their purposes closely from time to time. Other organizations give little thought to their purpose, assume that their purpose or purposes are generally understood, and seldom if ever undertake any systematic evaluation of purpose. Some organizations are created for one purpose and by accident or chance acquire a different purpose.

There are many considerations, and many complexities, involved in the definition of purpose within a productive enterprise. Presumably, purposes must be realizable, must be socially useful, must be technologically feasible, and must be possible of accomplishment from available resources. Purposes must command the allegiance of those who work within the organizational structure. Purposes must also be flexible and must be subject to adjustment in the face of environmental circumstances, of changing social needs or concerns, and of changing resources. Defining, clarifying, and modifying purposes are processes of some difficulty within organizational structures.

Organizational structure can influence purpose or purposes in varying ways. The traditions of an enterprise, the ideas of leaders, the concerns of persons working together within an organization, the responses of persons within an organization to the decision-making process—all of these factors can and do influence decisons about purpose and the accomplishment of purpose.

In spite of the many qualifications which surround the concept of purpose as an operation guidepost within organizations, the central fact remains that productive enterprises are purposeful structures, existing to produce some particular kinds of goods and services. An organization means purpose in action.

SPECIALIZATION OF WORK EFFORT. A second characteristic of organizational structure is work specialization. People working together generally have specialized tasks to perform, specialized roles to fulfill, specialized outputs to accomplish. Organization is in fact a bringing together of people who perform specialized work which adds up to a purposeful whole. Organizations are of necessity a social endeavor because people do specialize in the work they undertake.

Job specialization occurs in our economy and society because of at least four circumstances. First, individuals are different from one another in age, abilities, skills, and interests. Second, individuals who specialize in their work are more productive than individuals who endeavor to do any and all kinds of work. Third, individuals are different in their educational attainment and in the kinds of work they have learned to perform. And fourth, the technology of production processes tends to encourage work specialization because of differences in individual competencies and because of the objective of increasing work productivity.

A great deal has been written about job satisfaction in recent years, and the criticism has been made that some operatives on production lines obtain little job satisfaction from the repetitive performance of a very limited work assignment. Experiments have been conducted to broaden certain kinds of work specialization, and some increases in both job satisfaction and in worker output have been reported. But whatever the limitations of the assembly line, production engineers continue to find that work specialization does advance worker skill and worker output. Moreover, the alternative of general competence in place of specialized competence does not fit the fact of different competencies and interests among all the individuals who comprise the labor force.

Early in this century, the Bureau of the Census of the federal government devised a classification of occupations which it investigated by decennial censuses and by periodic sampling studies of civilian employment. The classification scheme has been revised or modified from time to time, and some shift occurs occasionally in the job classification of a particular kind of work. The major categories of jobs in this classification scheme are as follows:

Professional and technical.
Managers, proprietors, and administrators.
Clerical workers.
Sales workers.
Craftsmen, foremen, and skilled workers.
Operatives (including mine workers).
Laborers (except farm and mine workers).
Service workers (except domestic).
Domestic or private household workers.
Farm managers.
Farm foremen and workers.

This scheme for over 1,000 common occupational titles suggests the varied scope of the kinds of work that individual Americans are competent to perform and undertake to perform. Job specialization is an essential feature of the American economy and of American society. Training and educational programs help to strengthen the tendency toward job specialization. So also do the competencies and interests of individuals.

Organizational structures make use of job specialization. To a considerable extent organizational structures seek to accommodate job specialization. The objective of organization is to bring together persons of different job specializations who can, through their combined efforts, accomplish the purposes of the enterprise in turning out the desired goods and services.

WORK TECHNOLOGY. Just as work specialization is a common characteristic of organizations, so also is a defined process of work effort or of technology. Technology means simply a particular productive process, the process utilized to achieve an output of goods and services. Technology may make use of work specialization but it is not the same thing as work specialization. Work specialization is a job or task assignment. Technology is the process of achieving a desired output through a job assignment.

Many writers tend to mix their discussion of organizational structure with their discussion of management processes. Indeed, some commentators appear to find no distinction between the two. For example, considerable attention has been given to the subject of "the managing of organizations."

I believe there is a distinct and identifiable set of processes which can be labeled management. I shall say more about these concerns later. Here it is necessary to observe that a work process is not the same thing as a management process. A work process is the method or procedure utilized to produce the end products of an organization. A necessary condition or attribute of organizational structure is to accommodate and to facilitate the output of goods or services which a particular organization exists to produce.

The development of technology in an economy and in a society is the means employed to improve both the quality and the quantity of man's output. Technology involves tools and productive procedures. If man is to have more goods and services, and better goods and services, then man must make use of energy other than his own, and tools other than his hands. The whole history of Western man and of Western civilization is basically a history of an advancing technology, which has in turn made possible an advancing supply of goods and services for all persons.

It has been somewhat popular in the United States in the 1960s and 1970s to deride and criticize technology. It is true that some productive processes employed in American industry have been destructive of the physical environment of man and even of human, animal, and plant life. Some goods produced by our current technology have also been harmful to environment and to life. But if a particular set of production processes, or a particular set of products, has caused pollution of the environment and has threatened life, improved technology rather than the abandonment of technology may be the rational response.

In any event, the current design of productive processes within an organization may well influence or determine the relationship of people working together. Organizations do not invent technology; man determines technology. People working together make use of a productive process which may be new, or which may have evolved over time. And the relationship of people within an organization must necessarily accommodate a current productive technology.

An illustration of the impact of technology upon organizations may be drawn from the area of electronic data processing. The computer has made the storage, access, and analysis of information available to various persons in an organization. The organization must identify those persons who need access to current information or data processing in the performance of their work, and must decide how to provide such access on an effective and efficient basis. A good deal of experimentation by organizations has been necessary in order to accommodate the technology of electronic data processing.

One of the human relations aspects of organization is the complexity of introducing and utilizing new technological processes. Individuals who join a productive enterprise have been prepared by prior training or education for a particular kind of work process, or they receive on-the-job training in a current work process. As technology changes and as new work processes become available, the individuals who comprise an organization may be asked to undertake new work procedures. Individuals in an organization tend to feel comfortable with a work procedure that they learned and mastered at an early stage of their career. Persuading or motivating individuals to change their accustomed work procedures is likely to be a difficult endeavor. Many persons become anxious when asked to undertake new work processes. Some individuals welcome change in the routine of their lives; other individuals fear change from accustomed procedures.

The accommodation of technology is a continuing challenge to organizations and to the behavior of persons within an organization.

PATTERN OF COOPERATION. The human aspect of organization has been a subject of extensive interest for a good many years. Early discussions of organizational structure tended to emphasize three technical aspects of people working together: (1) the overriding attention to purpose, (2) work specialization, and (3) work technology. Organization was often viewed as a mechanistic arrangement to ensure accomplishment of intended work objectives (effectiveness) with ever-increasing work productivity (efficiency).

Gradually, scholars and experienced managers began to point out that organizations were made up of people, and that people brought their own particular interests and concerns to their organizational settings. As a consequence, there developed a new set of organizational concerns: the behavior patterns of the people who comprise an organization. More and more it came to be realized that there is a human aspect to organization, and that organizing work is more than an exercise in work specialization and work technology; organizing work is a social process of interrelating individuals to one another and a behavioral process of satisfying basic human concerns for status, reward, appreciation, and security.

Organizational structure provides a pattern of cooperation among people working together. In some discussions, organization is viewed as an external order imposed upon unwilling individuals by a "manager" who manipulates a process of rewards and punishments in order to ensure the desired behavior. The findings of social psychology suggest a different understanding. Organizations provide a structure of cooperative relationships among people who are motivated by job satisfaction and self-interest to work together.

Whatever its origins in pre-history, the division of labor between man and woman, between youth and adult, between hunter and grower, between settler and nomad, between farmer and city dweller, between soldier and priest, between clerk and ruler were rooted in social practice early on. Along with division of work developed patterns of cooperation and structures of interrelationship among people of tribe, community, and nation. People were joined together by a social cement more binding than the edict of authority or the fear of punishment. Cooperation became a way of life.

Organizations derive a basic characteristic from this disposition of individuals to work together. To be sure, in most organizational structures there is a system of rewards and punishments. Yet individuals are encouraged and motivated to work together by influences beyond the prospect of personal benefit or the threat of punishment. Individuals seek self-fulfillment, the satisfaction of personal interests and competencies, and the recognition of ability and achievement. Individuals work together in organizations because their personal goals can best be realized through cooperation with others, rather than through working and surviving as an individual.

Individuals develop patterns of behavior that necessarily influence organizational structure. We have noticed already that work habits and work traditions tend to become strongly ingrained in the organizational behavior of individuals. It is not unusual for individuals to become set in their ways and to be upset by the prospect or actuality of change. It is not unusual for individuals to expect increased personal satisfaction from their work performance over time. It is not unusual for individuals to compare their status and their remuneration with that of other persons or groups around them. All such inclinations are vital aspects of human nature found in the organization.

Sometimes the assertion may be heard in a group of persons coming together for a common purpose that "it is time for us to get organized around here." The implication in such an assertion is two-fold: (1) the need or desirability of joint action, and (2) the need or desirability for differentiated or specialized action. Organization thus expresses joint interest and particular tasks. Organization then becomes people working together in different ways to achieve a common purpose.

PATTERN OF MANAGEMENT. Organizational structure in a productive enterprise provides a pattern of management. Much of the writing about organization presents a description, and prescription, of hierarchical relationships among the persons who comprise the enterprise. This relationship is sometimes referred to as a "chain of command." The usual hierarchy is described as a pyramid, with a top manager, middle managers, supervisors, and workforce. The relationship involved in this hierarchy is one of superordination and subordination. Individuals have a boss; even the chief executive officer or top administrator has a board of directors or other authority to which he or she is responsible. In turn, managers supervise other persons who are subordinate to their direction.

The reality of organizational structure is usually more complicated than the theory of hierarchy would suggest. First, management in practice has tended to become collegial rather than individual. There are specialized competencies in management of an organization even as there are specialized competencies in work output. Many years ago, Arthur W. Macmahon and I developed the concept of "dual supervision" to describe the actuality of the management process in large organizations: a process of "general" supervision and a process of "specialized" supervision. Secondly, management processes have tended to become more participative as more individuals in an organization have acquired professional and technical competencies, as work processes have emphasized a shared understanding of shared purposes rather than command relationships, and as grievance procedures have become more widespread and more effective.

Chester Barnard, in his famous book *The Functions of the Executive,** pointed out that executives were usually careful not to issue instructions which they knew would not be carried out. (Barnard was a business executive, not an organizational theorist.) His words of managerial caution helped to encourage the whole school of thought generally referred to as the human nature of organization. More importantly, Barnard conveyed the actuality of management as concerned with people and their reactions as well as with work processes.

To some extent a pattern of management within an enterprise involves relationships of direction and supervision. Work specialization and work technology require some processes by which particular roles and particular tasks add up to intended outputs. The intended output must be decided and designed; the necessary resources for output must be brought together; the technology or work process must be determined; job specializations must be specified. And both the quantity and quality of work output must be measured or evaluated against planned performance. These tasks are often, and properly, described as the tasks of management. A pattern of management with the authority and responsibility

* Cambridge, MA: Harvard University Press, 1938.

to accomplish these tasks becomes one of the requirements of organizational structure in a productive enterprise. I have a very simple definition of management: management is work planning and work performance. In this broad sense many persons in an organization may be managers. Indeed, I would argue that the more professional and technical the personnel needed in a particular productive enterprise, the more likely are these persons to exercise various managerial tasks in work planning and work performance.

In attempting to develop a theory of organized endeavor (*Public Administration Review*, December 1967), I proposed a distinction in the work of an enterprise between operations and administration. Today, I would prefer to state this distinction as being between "output" programs and "support" programs. The purpose of an enterprise is the accomplishment or production of certain specified outputs; this production is accomplished by the performance of output programs and output units of the organizational structure. But these intended outputs can be accomplished only with the assistance of support programs and support units of an organization. These support programs are concerned with financial services, plant and maintenance services, logistical services (supplies and transportation), administrative services (communication, reproduction, and information processing), and personnel services (recruitment, safety and health, and grievances).

I would emphasize that management—that is, work planning and work performance—involves both output programs and support programs. Finding and maintaining the appropriate balance between the two kinds of endeavor is by no means a simple undertaking. Productive enterprises exist to accomplish outputs. Yet productive enterprises experience considerable pressures even to expand their support programs. It is necessary to remember that the costs of support programs are an overhead cost of the enterprise, a cost to be added to the direct cost of output programs.

Management direction means the authority to define, in some detail, the work objectives that the organized efforts of the enterprise are expected to accomplish. Management supervision means the authority to ensure that work objectives are in fact accomplished with the resources made available for the enterprise. The two processes of direction and supervision, of planning and performance, are interrelated and yet at the same time are different. Planning cannot be isolated from the practical concerns of performance. Performance cannot be isolated from the economic and social concerns of cost, usefulness, and demand. Management seems to be concerned above all else with achieving an appropriate balance between work planning and work performance.

There is still another dimension to management: the resolution of conflict. No matter how great or deep-seated may be the disposition in individuals to work together, there are also conflicts to be expected among individuals and groups of individuals. Rivalry and discord are organizational facts of life within most productive enterprises. Some individuals are dissatisfied with their jobs. Some individuals perceive their abilities as unrecognized, their performance as unappreciated. Some individuals resent any evidence of external authority. Some individuals resist any expectation or exhortation to change their usual behavior.

Groups of individuals with a perceived common interest may engage in rivalry with other groups. A group may believe that its assigned work output is too heavy or unreasonable. A group may feel that its status and prestige are being undermined by work assignments given to other groups, that its contribution to the output of the enterprise is not properly recognized, or that its role is threatened by changing circumstances over which it seems to have no control. For these and other reasons, organized groups or components of an enterprise may protest leadership recommendations and governance decisions.

The pattern of management within an enterprise seeks to prevent and to adjust to conflict, both conflict among individuals and conflict among groups. The ideal state of social behavior may be one of voluntary cooperation among individuals and groups. But the ideal state of social behavior is seldom if ever experienced in real life. Some conflict seems to be inevitable in most organizational settings. And conflict can on occasion be useful in promoting needed or desirable change in behavioral patterns. Many years ago, one perceptive organizational theorist, Mary Parker Follett, coined the phrase "constructive conflict" to refer to the discord among individuals and groups which led to innovation, to new processes, to new output, and to new accomplishment.

Organizational structure is a pattern of management in an enterprise, a pattern of work planning and work performance, a pattern for the accomplishment of output programs and support programs, a pattern for conflict resolution.

PATTERN OF GOVERNANCE. The writing about organizational structure in business enterprises has much to say about a decision-making process but very little to say about a structure of business governance. Governance is the authority and responsibility to make basic decisions about the purpose of an enterprise, the policies of an enterprise (such as pricing and quality of products), the programs of the enterprise, and the allocation of resources within the enterprise. These decisions are presumably the decisions of a board of trustees.

In his book *Management: Tasks, Practices, Responsibilities*, Peter F. Drucker * includes a chapter entitled "Needed: An Effective Board." Drucker believes that to portray corporate boards of directors as influential in decision making is a fiction, and he asserts that boards have become either management committees or ineffective groups. Furthermore, he insists that a board cannot be a useful governing body for a

* New York: Harper & Row, 1974.

corporation unless the board members serve full time. At the same time, Drucker argues strongly that corporations need a functioning board for three important reasons: (1) as a review organ to counsel, advise, and deliberate with top management, (2) as a mechanism to remove a top management that fails to achieve corporate goals, and (3) as an organ of public and community relations.

Many organizational structures of productive enterprises do include a board of directors or a board of trustees to perform the very kinds of tasks outlined by Drucker. Such an organizational arrangement is a pattern of governance. Moreover, there appears to be an increasing attention given to the governance role in organizational arrangements. Not long ago, the vice-chairman of the board of a large multinational corporation wrote that the most important task of the board was to ensure long-range strategic planning, and to make decisions based upon such planning. Recently, one large labor union in the United States declared that a major objective was to elect a member of the board of each company in the industry. A labor representative on corporate boards has become a fairly common practice in Western Europe. In the United States business corporations have been encouraged by federal government regulatory agencies to have a so-called "public" member on their boards of directors.

There are various reasons why increased attention is being given today to the pattern of governance in productive enterprises. These organizations are more than economic entities producing needed goods and services. In their pricing standards, quality standards, employment standards, compensation standards, production standards, expansion decisions, and location decisions productive enterprises are making determinations of far-reaching impact upon the social fabric, the economic well-being, and the political stability of the United States. The governance of productive enterprises (profit and nonprofit, goods producing and service producing) has become a critical matter, and organizations are necessarily giving greater concern to the arrangements for making decisions affecting the enterprise as a whole in relation to society.

PATTERN OF LEADERSHIP. Finally, organizational structure in a productive enterprise necessarily provides an arrangement for leadership. In much of the writing about business enterprise, top management and leadership are considered as synonymous. Actually, in corporate practice the designation of the chairman of the board of directors as "chief executive officer" suggests the leadership role which this officer is expected to fulfill. The chairman of the board on the one hand is expected to direct corporate planning, and on the other hand is expected to present recommendations to the board of directors for their action.

As I view the task of leadership in a productive enterprise, it is to provide the essential linkage between management and governance. Management must undertake the required planning, involving all managers of the organization in the process. The governance structure must make the decisions about purposes, policies, programs, and resources. Management is joined to governance by a structure and process of leadership.

For a time in the 1960s and 1970s, the whole concept of leadership suffered some eclipse in our society. John Gardner wrote in the mid-1960s that a whole generation of students had been innoculated with an anti-leadership vaccine. Gardner might well have applied his prescient observation to a whole generation of Americans, not just to a generation of students.

There is no need here to review the many reasons why leadership as an organizational arrangement came under a cloud. Warren Bennis wrote a book entitled *The Unconscious Conspiracy,** which had the suggestive subtitle: "Why Lead-

* New York: AMACOM, 1976.

ers Can't Lead." Bennis referred to the various pressures from many competing groups upon leadership attention, to the various efforts to prevent action on critical issues, to reluctance on the part of leaders to resign in support of moral principle, to the development of a culture stressing individual satisfaction without group obligation, to the loss of standards of individual integrity and commitment, to the "future shock" of rapid social change, to the demand that "open decisions" be "openly arrived at" (the meet-me-in-Macy's-window syndrome), and to the cultivation of popularity above responsibility. One may select what he pleases from such a list. Bennis was certain that whatever the cause or causes, those in leadership positions could no longer lead.

I would like to believe that since 1974 there has been some return to an understanding that organizations need leadership. And I would like to believe that more and more persons have come to realize that leadership cannot satisfy every individual and his interests, or meet all needs all the time. At the same time, I have come to believe that the leadership requirements of the 1980s and 1990s will be different from the requirements of the 1930s and 1940s. The United States is a larger and more complex nation, a nation uncertain of its resources for continued economic and other progress.

The new leadership is expected to define and articulate a social benefit from the purpose and program of productive enterprise. The new leadership is expected to be intelligent and informed as well as decisive. The new leadership is expected to be considerate of and in part responsible to the needs and aspirations of many internal and external groups. The new leadership is expected to encourage change which will be constructive, progressive, and humane. Somehow the organizational structure must provide a place for such leadership, must encourage the exercise of such leadership, and must evaluate the performance of such leadership.

THE UNIQUE CHARACTERISTICS OF ORGANIZATION

In the discussion thus far, our concern has been with common characteristics or attributes of organizational structure. We have passed by the intricacies of political structure in the United States. The common characteristics reviewed here have been those observed in operating the productive enterprises of our society and economy. We have been concerned with many different kinds of organizations: business enterprises, government agencies, military forces, voluntary associations, educational agencies, service enterprises, and others. To some extent, students, observers, and participants have found certain similarities, or at least certain common concerns, in organizing the relationships among people brought together to realize a common purpose. The common attributes of organizational relationship are patterns which recur in the many different social groupings undertaken to produce the goods and services useful to individuals.

If in fact these common characteristics do exist, as seems to be the case, then what about uncommon characteristics? Most "scientists" of social behavior look for repetitive and replicative patterns, and are inclined to regard deviations from such patterns as aberrations not subject to generalization. There is very little in the literature of organizational structures to suggest any common departures from or peculiarities of the observed patterns.

Actually every organizational structure is unique, even as every individual is unique. No two organized enterprises are ever identical. The varied leadership styles, the varied kinds of people brought together in an enterprise, the varied work technologies, the varied time factors and location environments—all such factors and others as well mean that every organized enterprise is different from any other enterprise.

The most important single difference is that of purpose. It is relatively simple to observe that organized enterprises have in common the formulation and pursuit of a stated purpose.

Insofar as it goes, any such statement appears to coincide with fact. It is quite complex, however, to observe that the purpose or purposes of every organized enterprise are different one from another. Purpose differs among types of enterprises. The purpose of a business enterprise is different from that of a military enterprise; the purpose of a labor union is different from that of a religious association; the purpose of a community recreation organization is different from that of a private foundation; the purpose of a hospital is different from that of a university; the purpose of a city police department is different from that of the U.S. Forest Service.

Very little attention in the literature of organizational structures has been given to the conditioning influence of purpose. One of the major objectives in this discussion is to provide a commentary on the conditioning influence of purpose upon the organizational structure of a university.

There are other conditioning influences in addition to purpose. Some of these influences have already been suggested: people, technology, and local environment. Purposes beget programs, and so programs are different among various kinds of enterprises and among particular enterprises. The external environment of economic, political, and social circumstances has its conditioning influence upon the number, the location, and the orgrnizational arrangements for enterprises. Purposes, programs, structures responsive to the social environment, financing—these common characteristics of organizational behavior are also the unique characteristics of organizational behavior. These unique characteristics condition the pattern of management, the pattern of governance, and the pattern of leadership within an organized enterprise.

It is the unique manifestations of organizational structure to be observed within the university which we shall be concerned to explore in this essay.

2

Purposes, Programs, and Structures

It has been traditional to describe the purposes of American colleges and universities as three-fold: (1) instruction, (2) research, and (3) public service. Several years ago one often heard purpose defined in terms of the preservation and transmission of knowledge, the advancement of knowledge, and the utilization of knowledge. The two sets of words embodied essentially the same concepts.

When the Carnegie Commission on Higher Education came to setting forth its thoughts on the subject in its report, *The Purposes and the Performance of Higher Education in the United States* (June 1973), the Commission used somewhat different words and a somewhat more elaborate scheme to suggest the scope of the higher education endeavor in our society. In this report the purposes of colleges and universities were stated as follows:

Purpose 1: The education of the individual student and the provision of a constructive environment for developmental growth.

PURPOSES, PROGRAMS,

Purposes	Out Programs

Instruction
  Self-Development
  Useful Employment
Research
  The Advancement of
    Knowledge
Creative Activity
  Artistic and Cultural
    Accomplishment
Public Service
  Demonstration
  Testing
  Continuing Education
  Advisory
Educational Justice
  Equality of Access
  Meritocracy
Constructive Criticism
  The Self-Renewal of Social
    Institutions
	Instruction
	  Field
	    Technical
	    Arts and Sciences
	    Professional
	  Levels
	    Associate
	    Baccalaureate
	    Graduate I
	    Graduate II
	    First Professional
	Research and Creative Activity
	  Centers
	  Projects
	Public Service
	  Centers
	  Projects
	Teaching Hospitals
	  Medical Care
	  Patient Care
	Independent Operations
	  Research and Public Service Centers
	Student Aid
	  Scholarships
	  Fellowships
	  Grants
	  Loans
	  Prizes
	Academic Freedom

AND STRUCTURES

Support Programs	Structures

Academic Support
  Libraries
  Educational Services
  Museums and Galleries
  Academic Computer Support
  Admissions
  Student Records
  Faculty Development
  Academic Management
 	
Student Services
  Learning Skills Development
  Counseling and Career Guidance
  Social and Cultural Development
  Recreation and Athletics
  Financial Aid Management
  Student Service Management
 	
Institutional Administration
  Executive Leadership
  Financial Management
  Administrative and Logistical Services
  Administrative Computer Support
 	
Plant Operations
  Building Maintenance
  Custodial Service
  Grounds Maintenance
  Utilities
  Repairs and Renovations
  Security
  Plant Management
 	
Auxiliary Enterprises
  Student Housing
  Student Food Service
  Faculty Auxiliary Services
  Student Health Service
  Intercollegiate Athletics
  Bookstore
 	
Transfers
  Mandatory
  Nonmandatory
	Campuses
	  Numbers
	  Size
	  Location
	  Public or Private
	
	Missions
	  Programs
	  Access
	  Enrollment Characteristics
	  Quality
	  Resources
	
	Governing Boards
	  Single Campus
	  Multi-Campus
	
	State-wide Boards
	
	Associations
	
	Federal Agencies

Purpose 2: Advancing human capability in society at large.

Purpose 3: Educational justice for the post-secondary age group.

Purpose 4: Pure learning—supporting intellectual and artistic creativity.

Purpose 5: Evaluation of society for self-renewal—through individual thought and persuasion.

In the elaboration of these general statements, the Carnegie Commission explained its intent by identifying certain critical issues and by suggesting certain broad lines of action. Thus the Commission asserted that a college could not "assume the full developmental responsibility for students." It urged more work and service opportunities for students, more attention to the career preparation interests of students, and a "greater mixing of age groups on campus."

In connection with the purpose of advancing human capability, the Carnegie Commission referred to research, public service, finding and developing talent, promoting geographical and occupational mobility, advancing levels of health care for people generally, providing educational and cultural opportunities for the public at large, and adding to the capacity of society to adjust to change. In terms of recommendations, the Commission proposed that federal research grants to higher education should be maintained at a level of 0.3 percent of gross national product. Support of basic research should be concentrated "on highly productive centers and individuals," while support of applied research should be subject to periodic reassignment. The Commission wanted public service "extended on a more even-handed basis to groups and persons," but warned that service efforts "should be appropriate to the educational functions of higher education." And the Commission desired that cultural and life-long learning facilities and programs should be made available to the general public on an expanded basis.

On the subject of educational justice, the Carnegie Commission asserted that the United States was the first nation ever formed with the declared intent of ensuring social justice to all citizens. At the same time, the report emphasized that the achievement of social justice was a responsibility of society as a whole, not an exclusive responsibility of education. The Commission supported universal access to higher education, but argued persuasively for the maintenance of qualitative standards according to the mission of the institution. The Commission urged that the total post-secondary age group should be a matter of public concern and that higher education be thought of properly as only one option. It also proposed that admission standards should be relaxed for members of disadvantaged groups, "provided that the chances are good that such students can meet graduation requirements in full." And the Commission recommended that special efforts should be made to find qualified members of minority groups and women for inclusion in the pool of candidates considered for faculty employment.

The Carnegie Commission pointed out that the college and university campus had become increasingly the locus for scholarship and creativity in our society. The Commission advocated increased federal government grant funds for the social sciences, humanities, and the creative arts.

Finally, the Carnegie Commission explained why it preferred the term "evaluation" rather than "criticism" as a major purpose of higher education. The Commission pointed to the continuing agenda of American life: the reduction of poverty, the elimination of discrimination based on race and sex, the reexamination of values, the renovation of cities, and the conservation of the environment. The Commission emphasized that the purpose of aiding society did not mean direct political action by institutions of higher education. The Commission argued that such direct political activity "could tear institutions of higher education apart internally," would often be counterproductive in achieving immediate aims and would lead to less support and more external controls, and would violate the principle of institutional neutrality that is essential to the political separation of higher education from the state.

The Commission pointed out that the purpose of government was to make good use of power, while the purpose of higher education was to make good use of the search for truth. The methods of social evaluation on the part of the university, said the Commission, should be the methods of careful thought, empirical evidence, logical argument, and persuasion offered to individuals and groups. The Commission declared that the principles of academic freedom for faculty members should be preserved and that the essential political independence of the campus should be fully protected by society. In addition, the Commission urged each institution to establish a policy of "self-restraint" against disruptive activities, improper use of campus facilities, improper political indoctrination of students, the selection and promotion of faculty members on the basis of political beliefs, and the commitment of the institution as an institution to any specific external political or social change.

As the Carnegie Commission looked forward to the year 2000, it anticipated continued conflict about the purposes of higher education, the need for institutions to reexamine and reassess their functions and performance, the desirability of eliminating functions "not directly tied to academic and educational activities," and a clearer differentiation of functions among campuses. In terms of conflict, the Commission identified three major issues to be resolved: (1) the role of higher education in the search for values, (2) the justification of commitment to the pursuit of new knowledge, and (3) the relationship of the university in supporting a particular social structure.

Insofar as the performance of higher education in general

was concerned, the Carnegie Commission rated the pursuit of pure scholarship and the advancement of human capability as superior; the educational advancement of students as "generally satisfactory . . . but with major improvements possible"; the promotion of educational justice as least adequate but with major improvements underway; the provision of an effective environment for student developmental growth as uncertain; and the critical evaluation of society as uneven.

The Carnegie Commission on Higher Education performed notable service to American society in its presentation and discussion of the purposes of higher education. It extended the scope of previous formulations by adding educational justice and critical evaluation of society to the listing of major purposes. It acknowledged the complexity of the relationship of higher education to society in America. It argued forcefully that the price of political independence for the university was political neutrality. It warned against the dangers of politicization of the university.

In two respects the Carnegie Commission discussion of 1973 appears in retrospect to have been deficient. It did not make a clear distinction between higher education service to particular students and clients and higher education service to society in general. Much more could have been said about the social obligations of the college graduate, and about the social benefits obtained from the presence in society of educated talent. Secondly, the Carnegie report said very little about the economic-political-social context within which colleges and universities operate. The report might, for example, have acknowledged that only a particular kind of society would permit higher education to seek political independence, and would tolerate critical evaluation of society and polity by the university.

No doubt the Carnegie Commission's report on purposes and performance was a disappointment to those students and those faculty members inclined to regard the university as a power base, as a launching pad for political demonstration and political demands. In its repudiation of a role of political activism for the university, the Carnegie report of 1973 may be said to have been a conservative document. In its sense of political and social realities the Carnegie report may be said to have been pragmatic and appropriate. At the same time, with the advent of the 1973 war in the Middle East, of the oil embargo of the Arab countries, and of economic recession, the social climate within which American higher education functions underwent considerable change, and American higher education began to experience considerable change as well.

PURPOSES

In our discussion we shall employ a somewhat modified version of the Carnegie Commission's formulation of purposes. We shall list these purposes as follows:

1. Instruction.
2. Research.
3. Creative activity.
4. Public service.
5. Educational justice.
6. Constructive criticism.

Each of these purposes deserves extensive discussion, and much more attention than is possible here. It seems desirable to separate creative activity from research, since the two purposes involve quite different endeavors, quite different processes, and quite different definitions of knowledge. Instead of the phrase "evaluation of society" we prefer the phrase "constructive criticism," but the concept is essentially the same.

Moreover, in our brief review of these basic purposes, our attention is focused internally rather than externally insofar as the university is concerned. Our attention is directed to what the university attempts to do within its "walls," within its own operational context. Obviously, the university seeks to fulfill these purposes because they realize a social as well as an individual benefit. This broader social benefit is only of incidental interest here. That broader social benefit will be considered in another and different discussion.

INSTRUCTION. Colleges and universities share in common the purpose of providing instruction to students. Such instruction generally embraces two primary goals: individual student self-development, and individual student preparation for useful employment in the nation's economy. There is a tendency for faculty members in the disciplines of the arts and sciences to assert that they are concerned mainly with instruction for student self-development. There is a tendency for faculty members in professional fields of study such as agriculture, business management, education, engineering, law, medicine, nursing, and social work to assert that they are concerned mainly with instruction for student useful employment. Both claims contain elements of truth, and both claims are subject to exaggeration.

Student self-development has various components: intellectual, creative, skill in either intellectual or creative performance, understanding and skill in interpersonal relationships, ethical commitment, commitment to civic virtue. It is probably accurate to say that faculty members have tended in this century to emphasize intellectual and creative development, along with skill in intellectual and creative performance. Understanding and skill in interpersonal relationships have been developed in large part in the residential institution and in extracurricular activities. Ethical commitment and commitment to civic virtue have appeared to be non-scientific and more closely related to religious faith and patriotic fervor than to intellectual exploration.

Student preparation for useful employment has been related to the development of professions in our economy, and more particularly to the emergence of a managerial, technological, and service economy. Professions, and paraprofessions, are knowledge based. They are involved in the application of knowledge to individual, productive, and organizational problems. Necessarily, professional and paraprofessional education requires a close relationship between professional practice on the one hand and educational preparation for practice on the other hand. The organization of this relationship, and the degree of influence to be exercised by professions over professional education, continue to be troublesome concerns.

The standard in para-professional and professional education has been quality of student development rather than responsiveness to labor market demand for educated talent. Universities cannot afford, however, to be indifferent to the job market, and in various ways have endeavored to adjust their standards of quality to employment opportunities.

Instruction, whether for the purpose of self-development or useful employment, is a process of interaction between a scholar/teacher and a student. The scholar/teacher can encourage, stimulate, and exemplify learning, but cannot compel a student to learn. A student learns by himself or herself. A student responds to the learning challenge provided by a scholar/teacher. A student reads books, makes use of other learning materials, enters into discussion, performs laboratory exercises, prepares papers, observes professional practitioners, and in turn improves his or her skills through practice and performance. The scholar/teacher does not produce or deliver learning in the customary meaning of those terms. The scholar/teacher promotes learning and competencies. The student learns, and becomes competent.

The opportunity for learning may be widely available in American society, as indeed it is, but not all young people and not all older people are motivated or are able to develop the capacity to learn that which is the stuff of higher education. The inescapable fact is that individuals in society have differential competencies to learn and to perform. Some educational psychologists assert that, in general, individuals differ in the speed of learning rather than in the competence to learn (this generalization excludes the mentally retarded). If we grant that there is empirical evidence of this fact, there still remain the factors of motivation and performance skill. Individuals, young adults and older adults, do not have the same interest, skill, and patience to learn.

A society that professes equality among individuals has some difficulty reconciling individual differences, including individual ability to learn. In attempting a reconciliation, a society must prescribe with care both its definition and its practice of equality. In higher education, the definition and the practice seek to achieve equality of educational opportunity, and to avoid discrimination based upon social status, economic status, race, religion, and ethnic background. Higher education acknowledges discrimination based upon motivation, competence, and performance. Higher education repudiates discrimination based upon any other criteria.

An unanswered problem of knowledge in American society is the source, or cause, of individual differences. It is generally acknowledged by biologists and psychologists that differences among individuals are both genetic and social. The exact relationship is still to be established. Certainly social circumstances may reinforce a genetic competence, or inhibit a genetic competence. And genetic competence is not evenly distributed among individuals within a particular race.

The important factor is that society benefits from the presence within its structure of individuals of educated talent. To be sure, only a fraction of young adults will complete a degree program. But that fraction may constitute the creative minority identified by Toynbee as indispensable to the survival and development of a civilization. In addition, the role of the individual of educated talent is to serve all citizens. The competence of a teacher, an artist, an engineer, a lawyer, a doctor, a nurse, a technician is a competence in the service of mankind. Instruction by a university of some persons as students has as its preeminent purpose service to all individuals. Universities have unfortunately too often failed to stress that quality of instruction is an asset to society, not simply a benefit to some particular individuals.

Instruction in American higher education as of 1980 is as much an art as it is a science. The art of teaching is a great art; there are many scholar/teachers who practice the art at a relatively modest level of skill. As an organization, the university puts instruction at the head of its list of purposes, seeks to recruit and retain scholar/teachers of competent skill in the art of teaching, and endeavors to establish an effective environment of learning. As an organization, the university can do little else.

RESEARCH. Research is a formalized process of advancing knowledge, and especially the process of advancing a particular kind of knowledge, empirical knowledge. For a long time in Western culture knowledge was relatively static, being derived from Greek and Roman classics and from treatises written in the major epochs of Western civilization (the Middle Ages, the Renaissance, and the Enlightenment). Knowledge was essentially synoptic, and scholarship was evidence of a capacity to deduce conclusions from first premises. Suddenly, especially in the seventeenth century, knowledge was proclaimed as derived from observation and experimentation, as based upon conclusions from induction or inference based upon perceived facts.

This revolution in knowing gained substantial headway in Western culture only in the nineteenth century, and historically was imported into America from German universities largely after 1860. Science as a way of knowing, and science as the foundation for technology and for service to society, made slow progress in the American university until World War II. The achievements of American science and technology in wartime—the atomic bomb, radar, the proximity fuse, and sonar were spectacular examples—gave a new impetus to research as essential to national defense and material welfare. New accomplishments in the health sciences, in space exploration, in communication, and in information processing after 1945 further enhanced the role of the American university as a source of useful knowledge through research.

Research fills a dual role in higher education and in society. Research demonstrates, or illustrates, that knowledge is dynamic rather than static, and that today's knowledge may be advanced by, or may be different from, tomorrow's knowledge. Secondly, research provides a knowledge base for the technology which may expand agricultural production, improve the health of individuals, offer new sources of energy, increase the supply of raw materials, diminish environmental pollution, and encourage the introduction of new and useful products and production processes. In addition, research provides the knowledge base for advancing man's understanding of social behavior and of social processes.

The scholar/researcher in recent years has tended to replace the scholar/teacher in prestige and status within the university. Some redress of this imbalance may well be underway as of 1980. Moreover, universities have often proclaimed the expectation that every scholar/teacher will also be a scholar/researcher, although considerable evidence exists that the scholar/researcher is to be found primarily in a limited number of research universities and that the scholar/teacher is not generally also a scholar/researcher.

Colleges and universities have feared that if they do not all embrace research as a purpose they will lose promising faculty members and will appear to be out of date in the knowledge faculty members profess. Only as the limitations of science have become more widely appreciated, and only as the mechanisms for updating the knowledge base of instruction have improved, has the distinction between instruction and research become more acceptable within higher education.

The university as an organization can embrace the research purpose only if its resources of outstanding scholar/researchers and of financial support for their research so permits. Research is expensive. Research requires a particular kind of academic talent. The supply of scholar/teachers is greater than the supply of scholar/researchers. And there is evidence that scholar/researchers flourish and are most productive when concentrated in a particular university setting.

CREATIVE ACTIVITY. In the jargon of higher education, creative activity means primarily the encouragement and sponsorship of the performing arts (music, dance, theater), the visual arts (painting, sculpture, and architecture), and creative writing. Colleges and universities have long included art, music, and theater as parts of their instructional purpose. The creative arts are both a subject of aesthetic understanding and appreciation and a field of achieving skill in performing through study and practice. As with research, only a few scholar/teachers in the creative arts become scholar/artists of distinction.

The whole subject of the artist in society—his or her development, encouragement, patronage, and recognition—is too complicated for brief discussion. It is sufficient to note that in recent years the patronage (financial support) of the creative artist has to a considerable extent been assumed by the American university. There remain other arrangements for support of the artist—the commercial theater and concert hall, the private nonprofit foundation, the government-subsidized artist or performing company—but increasingly the university has become the home of the artist.

The role of the scholar/artist within the university is three-fold: (1) to help all within the academic community have access to and acquire an understanding of the creative arts, (2) to help particular students develop their knowledge and skill as creative artists, and (3) to help students demonstrate their skill as creative artists. A few universities have included within their faculty individuals who have acquired considerable distinction as artists. Most if not all colleges and universities seek to include artists who can demonstrate the artistic achievements of our civilization and who can encourage the talented amateur, even if their own creative efforts fail to achieve general acknowledgment. The artist, whatever the state of his or her own creative talent, is a welcome participant in the American university.

As an organization, the American university may seek to include within its enterprise artists of distinction, and to encourage both their performance and the exercise of their creative talent. Again, artists of distinction and of creative talent are in short supply and are expensive to patronize. The effort to provide a favorable environment for creative activity nonetheless stands forth as a major purpose for many if not all universities.

PUBLIC SERVICE. Public service involves the American university in the activity of demonstrating and advising about the application of knowledge to current and continuing social problems. Perhaps the most celebrated of all public service endeavors has been the agricultural entension service of the land-grant university. Today, the teaching hospital of the university health science center is an even better example, although not so much the demonstration of health care as the delivery of health care has become its preoccupation. The updating of professional knowledge and skill in all professions is a part of the public service purpose. And demonstration of the individual satisfactions of knowledge and of creative achievement is a public service which may be extended to any and all interested individuals. To designate such demonstration as life-long learning is but to offer a new label for an old endeavor.

There are various complications in this public service purpose of the university. Shall public service efforts be subsidized socially, or paid for as consumer goods? What public service efforts shall be subsidized, and in what amount? What individuals and groups shall have access to university public service? How far beyond the scope of demonstration and advice shall the university go in performing public service? These questions have been troublesome for over 100 years, and are likely to be troublesome for many years to come.

The public service purpose of the university is vital in at least two respects. It is vital as a means of pointing out the utility of knowledge and of creative activity in adding to the sum total of material and other benefits derived by all of society from higher education. In addition, public service is an important means of interrelating the instruction of knowledge with the "real world" of practical concerns.

Research and instruction are illuminated by public service, by faculty contact with the individuals and organizations of society providing the economic, political, professional, and other goods and services essential to individual welfare. Contact with problems provides a stimulus to research and instruction. Contact with problems ensures that research and instruction are related to "real" concerns.

As an organization, the university seeks to recruit and retain faculty members competent to engage in public service, to obtain financial resources for public service projects and centers, and to ensure some "even-handedness" in the benefits conferred upon individuals and groups through public service.

EDUCATIONAL JUSTICE. The Carnegie Commission report in 1973 on higher education purposes and performance used the phrase "educational justice" to identify a major purpose of the American university. It is to be hoped that the phrase will acquire both general recognition as a major purpose and common currency in higher education discussions.

It is often overlooked that American higher education from its very beginning in 1636 espoused a revolutionary concept: that higher education should be open to individuals of talent and virtue regardless of social class. The two universities with which the English settlers of the American colonies were familiar were primarily Oxford and Cambridge, and both universities were principally available to the landed aristocracy and to the clergy. In the New World there would be some continuing evidence of this practice, but from an early date American higher education was revolutionary in nature.

Access to the university was never substantially utilized by young adults until after 1945. Yet such access was presumably available to all those who might desire it. The publicly sponsored college or university was committed to low tuition, and the privately sponsored college or university was committed to tuition at less than the cost of instruction, depending as they did upon endowment, gifts, and scholarships to ensure general access. Economic and social circumstances tended to discourage rather than to encourage access to higher education.

Even as the disposition of increasing participation by young adults became evident after 1945, greater attention began to be given to means for eliminating a limited access because of economic and racial characteristics. The mechanisms were two: (1) legislative and judicial decisions forbidding discrimination in admission based upon race, religion, national origin, and sex; and (2) government and other subsidy of individual students of limited economic means for meeting the personal costs of higher education. An expansion of higher education facilities and programs, primarily by public higher education, ensured that an expanding enrollment was accommodated in the 1950s, the 1960s, and the 1970s.

Educational justice has taken on an additional meaning besides that of equality of admission. The concept also embraces the policy and practice of nondiscrimination based upon race, religion, national origin, and sex in access to employment by colleges and universities, especially to employment as faculty members and principal administrative officers. Educational justice is both equality of access to admission and equality of access to employment.

At the same time, colleges and universities have sought to make it clear that equality of access does not mean equality of competence among all who may apply for admission or for employment. If standards of quality in higher educational performance are to be achieved, standards of competence must be observed in the admission of students and in the employment of personnel.

The doctrine of equality of access as the definition of the purpose of educational justice must necessarily be placed in juxtaposition with the doctrine of meritocracy. Nondiscrimination in access based upon race, religion, national origin, and sex is essentially a negative concept, a concept of appropriate morality in a multi-racial and multi-religious society of men and women of varied national origins. Meritocracy in access based upon individual competence is a concept of quality in higher education performance. Merit means standards in the pursuit of the purposes of higher education.

As an organization, the university promulgates policies and practices which seek to ensure equality of access founded upon individual merit. The quest is not easy, but it is a quest which gives meaning to the purpose of educational justice.

CONSTRUCTIVE CRITICISM. There is a little here which can be added to the Carnegie Commission's report in its discussion of the evaluation of society for self-renewal. It needs to be noted that the goal of survival for a civilization and for a national state rests insofar as the intelligence of man can determine upon the operative ideals of justice and of individual betterment. In our society, constructive criticism is a means to an indispensable social end. While freedom of the press, freedom of religion, and freedom of political association are vital forces in constructive criticism, so also is the American university.

The primary purpose of the university in the evaluation of society is to provide criticism founded upon thought. Other persons and groups may base criticism upon an appeal to emotion, upon dogmas of religious faith, upon a concern with self-interest. By the nature of its inherent commitment to rational thought and rational behavior, the university offers evaluation based upon knowledge and upon evident standards of creative expression.

Furthermore, the university is the forum or the marketplace for such evaluation, not the promulgator of a single definition of knowledge, a single standard of creative expression, or a single criterion for the application of knowledge and creativity to social performance. The university does not evaluate society, or offer constructive criticism of society. The university affords an opportunity for the individual faculty member to voice his or her evaluation, his or her criticism.

Criticism based upon thought can be destructive when it does not offer reasoned alternatives of behavior and institutional structure. Criticism is far easier to formulate and to offer than are alternatives. To be sure, criticism may be necessary as a prelude to the preparation of alternative courses of action. Yet criticism is essentially negative in scope and impact unless it is accompanied by reasoned choices for different efforts. Evaluation of society in terms of constructive alternatives remains the challenge to human intelligence, and to the university.

As an organization, a university seeks to articulate, protect, and defend a purpose of constructive criticism of social performance. A society of liberal democracy and of social pluralism can only be enriched and improved by such a purpose.

PROGRAMS

The programs of higher education are the means whereby the purposes of higher education are realized. Without programs, purposes lack operational reality. Without purposes, programs lack direction and utility. It is not enough for a university to state its purpose. The performance of the university must be judged by the effectiveness of its programs in accomplishing the avowed purposes.

Much could be said about the programs of the university. Programs involve centers of work planning, work budgeting and accounting, and work evaluation. Programs require resources of facilities, personnel, and income. Programs require management. Programs are the university in action.

At the beginning of this chapter, there is an outline of the principal categories of programs as commonly recognized in higher education. This outline is based upon a program classification structure developed by the National Center for Higher Education Management Systems and upon the uniform chart of accounts developed by the National Association of College and University Business Officers (NACUBO).

Without undertaking a discussion of the program outline, there are three items which do warrant some particular mention: (1) programs are divided into two categories: output programs and support programs; (2) student aid is included as an output program; and (3) auxiliary enterprises and income transfers are included as support programs.

In Chapter 1 we referred to the organizational characteristic in which some of the total effort of an enterprise is devoted to the desired outputs, while another part of the total effort is devoted to the maintenance of the enterprise as an organization. We chose to identify this second type of effort as the support programs of the enterprise, or as the overhead. No organized enterprise can hope or expect to accomplish its output without the requisite internal support.

In this respect a university is no different from any other organized enterprise. The university can accomplish its outputs of instruction, research, creative activity, public service, educational justice, and constructive criticism only if the necessary support in academic services, student services, plant services, institutional services, and auxiliary services is provided. Universities have problems in containing the rising costs of these support services, but this fact is no denial of the essential nature of the services themselves.

The categories of output programs enumerated here reflect the major purposes of the university. Public service has been subdivided to give special recognition to one particular kind of public service and one particular kind of research/ public service: the teaching hospital and the independent operation (research or public service) performed under contract with an outside agency. Because of peculiarities in financing these programs, the National Association of College and University Business Officers recommends their separate identification, and this recommendation makes management sense.

I list "academic freedom" as an output program when it might be more appropriate to mention constructive criticism of social evaluation as the actual service rendered. Academic freedom is a situation, a policy, a value-laden position. Yet the phrase is so often employed, the concept is so imperative, and the end so embedded in structural arrangements, that I have chosen to utilize the words simply to give emphasis to a familiar idea.

I have included student financial aid as an output program because this operation is one means of achieving equality of economic access for students to instructional programs, and because this program translates into reality the purpose of educational justice in student admissions. In my judgment, it is erroneous to envisage the program and the costs of student aid as a student service. The program and the costs are a way of realizing a vital purpose of higher education in our society.

Auxiliary enterprises have been identified as a separate organizational support program in accordance with the recommendation of the National Association of College and University Business Officers. Once again peculiarities of financing, as well as the scope of these services at the residential college or university, justify such identification.

Finally, a program of transfers of income from current operations to debt service accounts, to loan fund accounts, and to reserve accounts should be separately indicated. If anything, it seems evident that colleges and universities under the pressures of demands for current operating expenditures have given too little attention to transfer policies and to transfer programs. The least that can be said here is to point out the desirability of inclusion in the program outline, an inclusion again acknowledged by NACUBO.

STRUCTURES

The basic structural unit of higher education is the campus. The campus is a particular facility in a particular location bringing people together to offer instruction and perhaps other output programs of higher education. A campus may be a single building in a large city; it may be a number of buildings connected by streets and walks within a city, a small town, or a rural area; it may be large or small. A campus is a geographical location and a set of higher education programs. From its campus setting, a university may offer off-campus instruction. The essential difference between a campus and an off-campus center is a matter of arrangement. The off-campus center often makes use of rented facilities and lacks the attribute of permanence; the off-campus center tends to provide limited instructional programs or courses and lacks the attribute of comprehensive scope; the off-campus center draws its faculty resources from the campus or from the community on a part-time basis and lacks the attribute of full-time faculty operation.

Currently there is a great deal of controversy about off-campus centers. There is a suspicion that some campuses undertake off-campus instruction to augment income rather than to provide an essential service. There is a suspicion that off-campus instruction tends to be of poor quality and to deny students the full benefit of campus resources and opportunities for self-development. And there is often considerable competition among off-campus centers located in the same city, with attendant evidence of "cut-throat" practices demeaning to the integrity of higher education.

The 1978-79 directory of colleges and universities published by the National Center for Educational Statistics listed 3,173 identifiable campuses for the United States and certain outlying areas (Puerto Rico, Virgin Islands, the Canal Zone, Samoa, Guam, and the Pacific Trust Territory). These campuses were classified according to whether they were publicly controlled or privately controlled, whether they offered four-year or two-year programs, and by location (states, the District of Columbia, and outlying areas).

The Carnegie Council on Policy Studies in Higher Education in 1976 published a revised classification structure of colleges and universities in the United States. This classification structure is summarized in Table 1, which shows the number of institutions in each category. The table does not include the sub-groupings for research universities, doctorate-granting universities, comprehensive universities, and liberal arts colleges intended to indicate the magnitude and quality of institutional activities.

The distribution of student enrollment in 1976 is summarized in Table 2.

Tables 1 and 2 clearly indicate the variety of types of institutions which comprise the structure of higher education, or of "university" education, in the United States as of 1976. The predominance of public higher education institutions in relation to private higher education institutions (except in

Table 1. The structure of higher education in the United States, 1976.

	Public	Private	Total
Doctorate-granting institutions			
Research universities	62	36	98
Doctorate-granting universities	57	29	86
Comprehensive universities	354	240	594
Liberal arts colleges	11	572	583
Specialized institutions			
Theological seminaries	0	270	270
Medical schools	32	19	51
Other health profession schools	1	25	26
Schools of engineering	8	438	46
Schools of business	1	33	34
Schools of fine arts	5	50	55
Schools of law	1	15	16
Teachers colleges	3	25	28
Other	19	15	34
Two-year colleges	909	238	1,147
Nontraditional institutions	3	3	6
Total	1,466	1,608	3,074

SOURCE: Carnegie Council on Policy Studies in Higher Education, *A Classification of Institutions of Higher Education*, revised edition, 1976.

liberal arts colleges and specialized institutions) is obvious. It is not necessary to review the criteria employed in this classification scheme, or to elaborate the differences among the various categories of institutions. We shall consider the subject of differences in the mission of various institutions in Chapter 3. Insofar as location is concerned, we may note that colleges and universities are dispersed throughout the 50 states and the District of Columbia. The largest number of institutions tend to be located in the most populous states, but some states of modest population size have several public institutions. Only Wyoming had a single public university, seven public two-year colleges, and no private colleges or university.

Table 2. Distribution of student enrollment (in thousands).

	Public	*Private*	*Total*
Doctorate-granting universities	2,389.0	673.4	3,062.4
Comprehensive universities	2,372.6	769.9	3,169.5
Liberal arts colleges	19.5	511.7	531.2
Specialized institutions	137.9	277.9	415.8
Two-year colleges	3,825.2	152.8	3,978.0
Nontraditional institutions	12.4	1.7	14.1
Total	8,750.6	2,414.4	11,164.0

Table 3. Average enrollment of U.S. colleges and universities, 1976.

	Public	*Private*
Doctorate-granting universities	20,076	10,360
Comprehensive universities	6,703	3,321
Liberal arts colleges	1,818	895
Specialized institutions	1,971	567
Two-year colleges	4,208	643
Nontraditional institutions	4,133	567

The average enrollment of each type of institution is shown in Table 3.

The distinction between public and private colleges and universities (except for theological seminaries) is not so much a distinction between programs offered as it is a difference in enrollment size and in financing. The data summarized in Table 3 show that the average enrollment size of private institutions tends to be smaller than that of the public institutions. Indeed, among the nearly 600 private liberal arts colleges enumerated by the Carnegie Council, our own calculation is as follows:

Enrollment Size	Number of Institutions
3,000 and over	1
2,000 to 2,999	16
1,000 to 1,999	198
Less than 1,000	357
Total	572

Small size would appear to be a major difficulty for private liberal arts colleges.

In addition, the private college and university, except for research support and student aid support, must depend upon income from charges to students and from philanthropy. The public college and university, except for research support and student aid support, must depend for income upon charges to students and from government subsidy (primarily state government subsidy).

In general, colleges and universities in America are governed legally by a board of trustees or a board of regents (occasionally other designations are employed). The principal characteristics of governing boards are lay (rather than educational) membership, part-time (even occasional) service, unpaid service, authority and responsibility for selecting the campus president, final authority on policy and budget and personnel actions, and substantial dependence upon professional advice (especially that of the campus president).

The governing board of a private college or university is usually self-perpetuating, although some members may be selected by an alumni association and other members by a church-related body. Board members serve for such period of time as may be prescribed by the by-laws. Board members represent the "public" interest in the operation of the college or university as they may be disposed to define or articulate that interest. The governing board seeks to defend and perpetuate the institution to the fullest extent possible, to maintain a certain balance among the internal constituent groups of the institution, and to augment the financial resources of the institution.

The governing board of a public college or university is usually appointed by the governor of a state, with approval by the state senate. Board members serve overlapping terms as prescribed by state law. Board members represent the state government interest in the operation of the public college or university, exercising authority which may be executive, legislative, and judicial in nature. The governing board is an insulating mechanism to blunt "political" domination or influence upon the public college or university. At the same time, the governing board assists in the public advocacy of government financial and other support for the college or university.

A unique characteristic of the public governing board is its multi-campus jurisdiction. In 21 states all "senior" public colleges and universities were governed in 1979 by a statewide governing board. The number of senior public colleges and universities in these states ranged from three to 16. In the 29 other states, there were multi-campus systems of senior public colleges and universities under a single governing board in 19 states. Altogether, of the 473 state universities identified in the Carnegie Council data presented above, 143 had a single governing board, while 330 state universities were part of a multi-campus system.

The multi-campus governing board emerged within state governments from two primary factors: (1) the push of state universities to establish additional campuses in major urban areas of a state, and (2) the emergence of teachers colleges formerly governed by a state board of education as state universities but now under a multi-campus governing board. The multi-campus governing board presents problems of professional leadership and of diversity in handling the circumstances of individual campuses.

In states where there is not a state-wide governing board, and in four states with such governing boards, a state board of higher education has been created by law or by constitutional prescription. The state board of higher education does not have governing authority over individual campuses but has some authority as a planning and coordinating body. The extent of this authority varies from state to state.

Both state-wide governing boards and state boards of higher education confront a critical problem in developing their political relationship to a state governor and state legislature. On the one hand, these boards endeavor to avoid partisan political pressures harmful to the mission and integrity of public higher education. On the other hand, these boards seek to offer professional advice about higher education needs to the governor and legislature. Basic policies about the scope and support of state colleges and universities must be made by the state government. The handling of this delicate political relationship of insulation and of dependence has taxed both the organizational thinking and the leadership competence of persons in public higher education.

Even though their enrollment tends on the average to be smaller than that of the public colleges and universities, the private colleges and universities offer an alternative to public higher education. In addition, some private colleges and universities establish standards of quality which serve to inspire and assist the performance of public colleges and universities. Without the example of private colleges and universities, public colleges and universities might fare poorly in their relationship to state government.

It is possible here only to mention the existence of the many associations of colleges and universities in the United States: state associations, regional associations, regional accrediting associations, associations of professional colleges and programs, an association of older state universities, an association of other state universities and colleges, an association of leading research universities, an association of independent (private) colleges and universities, an association for liberal learning, an association of community colleges, an association of institutions in general. All of these and other similar associations have some role in exchanging experience and information among colleges and universities, in developing and enforcing standards of quality, in formulating policy positions, and in providing services of various kinds.

One must also mention the major private foundations in the United States which provide grants for research, innovation, and general development for the benefit of both public and private colleges and universities—bodies such as the Ford Foundation, the Rockefeller Foundation, the Carnegie Corporation, the W. K. Kellogg Foundation, the Mellon Foundation, and the Lilly Endowment. Foundations sponsored and supported by business corporations have also been helpful—bodies like the Exxon Educational Foundation, the U.S. Steel Foundation, and others.

Finally, no account of the structure of colleges and universities would be complete without acknowledgment of the major role of federal government agencies—especially the Department of Education, the Veterans Administration, and the Social Security Administration—in providing grants and loans to students to assist them in meeting the personal costs of higher education enrollment; and also the National Institutes of Health, the National Science Foundation, the Department of Energy, the Department of Defense, and the National Foundation for the Arts and Humanities in providing grants to colleges and universities for research and creative activity.

CONCLUSION

Obviously, the purposes, programs, and structure of higher education in the United States entail extensive operation and extensive organizational arrangements. No one interested in the performance of colleges and universities in general, or in a particular college or university, can afford to be ignorant of or unconcerned with this complex interrelationship of purpose, programs, and structure.

Higher education as a social institution of more than 3,000 separate enterprises seeks to fulfill the needs and interests of individuals in learning, and to fulfill the needs and interests of society in having persons of educated talent available for the managerial and professional service required in a highly technical economy and polity. Higher education is a unique social institution in the purposes it seeks to provide, in the programs it seeks to accomplish, and in the structure it maintains to deliver its educational products.

There is no comparable set of purposes, programs, and structure simply because there is only one social institution of higher education and only one array of some 3,000 enterprises established to provide higher education. But an introduction to purposes, programs, and structure is only the beginning of an effort to comprehend the unique organizational characteristics of the university as an enterprise.

3

Essentials
of Mission

Individual colleges and universities are expected to have statements of mission, and periodically to revise or update such statements. Statements of mission are supposed to indicate the general purpose which a campus exists to achieve. Unfortunately, many statements of mission are so general that they are almost meaningless. Statements of mission are supposed to indicate the distinctive characteristics which make a particular campus different from other campuses. But many colleges and universities are fearful of being distinctive, and so tend to suggest that they are just as purposeful, and just as good, as any other college or university.

Within public higher education, state-wide governing boards or state boards of higher education require all state-supported colleges and universities to prepare a statement of mission. One of the failures in this process is often the absence of any guidelines indicating what the state board expects in terms of content for a statement of mission. Most governing

ESSENTIALS OF MISSION

Instruction
    Objectives
      1. General education
      2. Career and professional education
      3. Civic virtue
    Programs
      Technical
      General education
      Arts and sciences: undergraduate
      Professional: undergraduate
      Arts and sciences: graduate I, graduate II
      Professional: graduate I, graduate II
      First professional: law, medicine, dentistry, osteopathic
        medicine, optometry, veterinary medicine, theology
Research
    Major interest
    Secondary interest
Public Service
    Continuing general education
    Continuing professional education
    Clinics
    Museums and performing arts
    Consulting services
Orientation
    Residential
    Urban
Access
    Open admissions
    Selective admissions
    Educational justice
Enrollment Size
    Limited
    Stable
    Expanding
    Contracting
Enrollment Characteristics
    Full-time versus part-time
    Residential versus commuting
    Preponderantly white, preponderantly black
    Church-related versus nonsectarian
Quality
    Standards of access
    Standards of performance
    Standards of input resources
    Evaluation of outcomes and performance
Resources
    Pattern of income
    Pattern of resource allocation
    Capital assets: plant and endowment

boards of private colleges and universities expect the enterprise they "govern" to have a statement of mission. Accrediting associations and bodies expect a college or university to have a statement of mission. Again, in both of these instances very little has usually been provided in the way of specification about the scope or specific content desired in a statement of mission.

In the "good old days," the president of a college or university often undertook to articulate a statement of mission on his or her own initiative with little or no assistance from any administrative associate or faculty colleague. In the years before 1940, the president seldom enjoyed the luxury of an extensive administrative staff, and the president was expected not only to represent the college or university as a whole but also to have a vision of the college or university which no one else was likely to possess. Moreover, in the good old days, statements of mission were often considered of little importance. If the president wished to tinker with words and offer a splendid version of college or university endeavor, few were disposed to be critical.

In the years since 1960, the writing of statements of mission has become an exercise in consensus building for faculty, students, administrative officers, trustees, and government officials. The accepted procedure is to appoint a committee to prepare a statement of mission, and the resulting product resembles any product produced by a committee: the lowest common denominator of shared interest. In the absence of strong presidential leadership—and such leadership was often suspect in the decades of the 1960s and 1970s—faculty interests tended to dominate the preparation of mission statements. And faculty members, perhaps because of the limitations of their own graduate education, were likely to set forth aspirations appropriate to perhaps ten or twenty of the leading universities in America. To set forth any lesser aspiration was to accept the proposition that faculty members of the university were not so "good" as faculty members in some other university. No faculty member wished to be classified as inferior to any other faculty member, within a particular campus or within the United States.

The common failures in statements of mission have led some academic administrators and observers to conclude that the entire effort to formulate descriptions of purpose is a waste of time and effort. These critics would not necessarily abandon statements of mission but would place less emphasis upon their importance. It has even been suggested that statements of mission should give way to statements of program objectives and of program performance. The old adage is suggested that the actions of a college or university speak louder than its words. This last suggestion is not without some merit.

Personally, I am inclined to believe that statements of mission are not so much useless as misused. The goal in preparing a statement of mission should be understood as endeavoring to define the distinctive characteristics of a college or university rather than the common characteristics shared by higher education enterprises in general. We can take for granted that faculty members are committed to instruction, research, and public service. We can take it for granted that faculty members believe in academic freedom. We can take it for granted that faculty members desire generous compensation and comfortable working conditions. The problem in formulating a statement of mission for any particular campus is not how to articulate these general commitments and interests. The problem is how to indicate that a particular campus has particular commitments and interests.

I believe that the path to meaningful statements of mission is through agreement about the scope and content of such statements. The outline presented at the beginning of this chapter is intended to provide one person's proposal about the desirable scope and content of a statement of mission. The discussion which follows is an elaboration of that outline.

It should be pointed out that one of the first problems that confronts any analyst of higher education enterprises in the United States is how to describe the variety and diversity of campus missions. The Carnegie Commission on Higher Education, in its extensive study from 1967 to 1974, faced this problem, and its response was a fairly elaborate classification scheme intended to suggest differences in mission based upon programs and based upon quality. Quality was judged primarily by the volume of federally funded research and by average test scores of incoming freshmem.

The Carnegie Commission's classification was generally useful insofar as it went. The number of categories was probably as many as could be conveniently employed for analytical use. But the classification scheme could not begin to suggest the wide-ranging reality and opportunity for distinctive endeavor among the 3,000 higher education campuses in the United States.

TWO BASIC DISTINCTIONS

At the outset of this discussion we need to acknowledge two basic distinctions of campuses, which are not included in the outline at the beginning of this chapter. One basic distinction was mentioned earlier: the distinction between public and private enterprises. The distinction is important in terms of financing, enrollment size, and response to social expectations. The second basic distinction occurs within the private sector of higher education: the distinction between secular (or nondenominational) colleges or universities and church-related enterprises.

Several years ago, the American historian Richard Hofstadter identified the thrust to secularization as a major development in higher education late in the nineteenth century and continuing into the twentieth century. In the 1800s many so-called state universities had clergymen as presidents, most of whom were Protestants. Only after the Civil War were more and more presidents of state universities laymen and educators rather than clergymen. In the private colleges that became universities after 1870, presidents tended to be drawn from faculty backgrounds and were no longer clergymen. Some private colleges, especially those preparing undergraduates to enter graduate education and graduate professional education, divested themselves of their religious affiliations. The concern for scholarship and scientific knowledge was perceived as being somehow inhibited by religious faith and dogma. Secularization of learning became a sign of commitment to learning.

Yet as late as 1978, some 784 privately controlled colleges and universities out of a total of nearly 1,600 nonprofit higher education enterprises listed themselves as having some degree of affiliation with a religious denomination. Some 500 declared an affiliation with Protestant denominations, some 200 declared a relationship to the Roman Catholic Church, 24 had an affiliation with the Jewish faith, and 15 indicated ties to "other" religious bodies.

The relationship may vary from outright "ownership" of a college or university by a religious denomination or religious order to a vague kind of affiliation or "sympathetic association" between a religious denomination and a college or university. These ties are not severed largely because of college or university dependence upon some amounts of financial support flowing directly or indirectly through church channels.

If a college or university, public or private, accepts any government support for its operation or for its students, the enterprise is forbidden by law to discriminate in admissions or in employment upon the basis of religion. In practice, a college or university may actively seek students and staff in terms of religious affiliation, even if overt discrimination is illegal. Faculty members in religiously affiliated colleges or universities tend to resist any form of religious dictation of their scholarship, and religious faith as such appears to be less and less important each decade in the instructional programs of these enterprises.

Religious affiliation cannot be ignored as a factor in the financial support of some colleges and universities, and even as an influence upon student and staff recruitment. But increased public support of private colleges and universities and of their students is tending to ensure the gradual disintegration of formal ties between organized religion and higher education.

The one exception to this generalization is of course the theological seminary, which is the professional education arm of religious denominations. Seminaries and their students do not receive financial support from governments, and remain closely tied to religious denominations.

INSTRUCTION

In any statement of mission for a college or university, first attention is necessarily given to its instructional purpose. There are at least two major components to an instructional mission: (1) general objectives, and (2) particular degree programs.

The general instructional objectives of a college or university may be to provide a general education, to provide career and professional education, and to cultivate individual standards of "civic virtue." Most colleges and universities will assert their commitment to all three objectives. The test of such commitment is to be found in performance, in actual practice.

The Harvard report of 1945 * defined general education in terms of the following desired competencies on the part of students: "to think effectively, to communicate thought, to make relevant judgments, to discriminate among values." The report propounded a "theory of general education" which included comprehension of the Western intellectual heritage, appreciation of individual life "as a responsible human being and citizen," awareness of "areas of knowledge," commitment to particular "traits of mind," and devotion to the attributes of good citizenship.

In its 1977 report on missions of the college curriculum, the Carnegie Foundation for the Advancement of Teaching declared: "General education is now a disaster area." The report went on to assert that the concept of general education was on the defensive and had been losing ground for more than 100 years. Few persons acquainted with the realities of American higher education would be disposed to quarrel with this judgment. We cannot begin here to review the immense body of writing on general education, or the reasons for the failure to find appropriate means to a noble end. Yet American colleges and universities continue to profess general education as a major instructional purpose.

Career and professional education—instruction to enter a selected field and to acquire skill as a practitioner—has been a major purpose of higher education since the days of the medieval university. American higher education probably achieved its zenith in career and professional education in the decades from 1945 to 1975. But in the 1970s, surpluses of graduates in professions began to appear in the American labor market, and such surpluses seem likely to continue throughout the 1980s. In an acute form, American colleges

---

* *General Education in a Free Society* (Cambridge: Harvard University Press, 1945).

and universities have had to confront the issue of the appropriate relationship between professional education and opportunities for professional employment.

Most faculty members and most administrators in colleges and universities acknowledge an affective dimension to their instructional endeavor, but there is little agreement about the desirable object of this emotional obligation or impulsion. One possible object is civic virtue: a cultivation of and commitment to values involving the dignity of man, increased tolerance of others, restraint from conduct harmful to others, respect for property, devotion to due process, and subscription to social pluralism and liberal democracy. Colleges and universities in America have begun once again to attempt a reconciliation between reason and values. In turn, this effort is being reflected in statements of mission.

The general objectives of instruction are accomplished through degree programs. These degree programs vary by areas or subjects of specialization and by levels of specialization. Insofar as areas or subjects of specialization are concerned, the familiar categories are technical education, the arts and sciences, and professional education. I add general education as a subject of specialization because sometimes the general objective of general education is reflected in a particular degree program. Insofar as the levels of specialization are concerned, the customary ones as identified by degrees are as follows:

Associate Degrees (two years)
    Technical education
    General education
Bachelor's Degrees (usually four years)
    General education
    Arts and sciences
    Professional

Graduate I, Master's Degrees (one to two years)
   Arts and sciences
   Professional
Graduate II, Doctoral Degrees (two to four years)
   Arts and sciences
   Professional
First Professional (three to four years)
   Dentistry
   Law
   Medicine
   Optometry
   Osteopathic medicine
   Theology
   Veterinary medicine

The usual assumption is that the higher the degree (bachelor's degree compared with an associate degree, doctoral degree compared with a master's degree), the more highly specialized is the knowledge expected of the degree recipient, and the more highly skilled is the competence of the degree recipient. Much of higher education instruction is organized on the basis of increasing specialization and depth of knowledge along with increased skill of the individual in the pursuit of knowledge or in the application of knowledge. Degrees thus represent specialization of knowledge and depth as well as skill in knowledge.

In this arrangement, membership in a graduate faculty presumably signifies greater experience and skill in knowledge than membership in an undergraduate faculty. The number of faculty members competent to offer degree instruction at the graduate level is presumably much smaller than the number competent to offer degree instruction at the associate or bachelor's degree level. Moreover, the workload of the faculty member at the graduate level is different from the workload of the faculty member at the undergraduate level. The graduate faculty member is expected to be a scholar/researcher; the undergraduate faculty member is expected to be a scholar/teacher. These differences are likely to be reflected in differences in compensation and in differences in the costs of instruction per student.

There are other differences in cost which arise in degree programs. As a general proposition, degree programs in the biological sciences, physical sciences, architecture, engineering sciences, and the health professions tend to cost more at all levels of instruction than degree programs in the humanities, the social and behavioral sciences, business administration, education, and law. The reasons have to do with smaller enrollments, the extensive use of equipment, and smaller student-faculty ratios.

Because of limitations in available financing as well as because of reduced enrollments, colleges and universities will necessarily have to give greater attention in the 1980s than in the 1960s and 1970s to the degree programs they offer. Colleges and universities already tend to differ in the degree programs they offer. They may have to become even more distinctive in the years ahead. Degree program distinctions will be reflected in the instructional mission of a particular college or university.

RESEARCH

The research mission of a college or university may be a major interest or it may be a secondary interest. The difference will depend upon facilities, faculty abilities, income, and, in the instance of public institutions, state government planning. Because they have often received their graduate education in leading research universities, many faculty members enter their academic career enamored of research. Research has been a principal pathway to academic recognition in the past 30 years. Research has captured the public mind and enjoyed considerable political support. Research has been socially useful. Research has advanced knowledge.

There are limitations to the research mission, however. Research is expensive. And, in spite of the general aspirations of many faculty members, only a few are destined to become outstanding research scholars. Only a few faculty members become creative artists, and only a few become professional practitioners of distinction. Because of the great expense and because research scholarship seems to flourish in a university environment where research is a primary mission, research activity tends to be concentrated in the setting of a research university.

The expense of research needs recognition and emphasis. Most research projects and activities are financed by grants from the federal government. As helpful (indeed, as indispensable) as federal grants are in encouraging and providing for research, they seldom cover all the costs. Often federal granting agencies expect, or demand, a university contribution to research activity. Only the private university with a substantial and expanding endowment or the state university with a substantial subsidy from state government for this particular mission can afford to be a research university.

If the mission of a university includes research as a major or primary interest, there is no reason why research cannot and should not be a secondary interest at other colleges and universities. Many colleges and universities have faculty members competent to undertake research projects and interested in doing so. To the extent that separate financial support can be obtained for such research effort, or some modest amount of general income can be set aside for the purpose, these faculty members may well be encouraged to undertake research activity.

It needs to be emphasized also that research is an essential part of learning. Not only is research a component of learning at the graduate level, but research is also a component of faculty development throughout an academic career. Knowledge in our time is not static. Because the means of communication are extensive today, faculty members can and do remain current in the knowledge they instruct throughout their academic career. Some first-hand experience in research may, however, enhance this capacity for faculty development.

A college or university may have only a secondary interest in research, but it is to be hoped that the research interest is secondary, not nonexistent. Even the community college which is proud of the primacy of its instructional mission can still afford to give some incidental attention, and encouragement, to faculty research.

Much of what has been said here about research applies especially to the biological and physical sciences, to mathematics, and to the health and engineering sciences. To a lesser extent, because the problems are different and the methods of discovery more diverse, research in the social and behavioral sciences is somewhat different. Research in the humanities is also somewhat different.

In addition to research, however, a college or university may have the mission of encouraging and promoting creative activity in literature, the visual arts, and the performing arts. Such encouragement is expensive, and can be undertaken only to the extent that both special grants and general support make it possible.

Research and creative activity are indispensable to the vitality of higher education in America and are an essential part of the higher education mission, whether or not the mission is a primary interest and whether or not the mission is a secondary interest.

PUBLIC SERVICE

The public service mission of a college or university is essentially one of translating knowledge into practice and translating artistic competence into performance. The public service mission may involve various kinds of activities and projects, such as an agricultural extension service, an urban extension service, adult continuing general education, adult continuing professional education, testing and advisory services, clinics and teaching hospitals, galleries and museums, theater and performing arts, and public broadcasting.

Public service integrates instruction and research with the practical problems that are of importance to individuals, to groups, to businesses, and to governments. The practical problems of everyday life illuminate the needs for instruction and research. The application of knowledge in the solution or amelioration of practical problems underlines the social utility of higher education. Similarly, the preservation and display of works of art, the exhibition of historical and other artifacts, and the performance of music and dance and other talents enrich cultural competence and understanding in society at large.

Many faculty members are quite interested in the practical application of their knowledge or in the performance of their creative talent. One policy problem to be resolved on a campus is the extent to which full-time faculty members shall practice their abilities off campus, and the extent to which faculty members shall make use of college or university facilities in public service for which they receive personal remuneration.

Two issues complicate the public service mission of a college or university. One issue is that of how public service projects and activities shall be paid for. The second issue is the scope and extent of the public service effort. Both issues relate to the mission of the institution.

If a university insists that its public service mission shall be restricted to the income provided by government sources or generated by the activities themselves, then the scope and extent of the mission are determined by the financial resources of the institution. In such a mission a university serves those who can pay for the service, or those for whom the government is willing to pay.

It must be recognized that the public service mission of higher education is basically a demonstration mission. The role of higher education in society is not to displace other social institutions and enterprises, such as the family, businesses, professional practitioners, community health services, community and commercial agencies for the performing arts, voluntary groups, and government agencies. The role of higher education is to inform all these other enterprises of the knowledge and skills available to them in the performance of their essential services.

Colleges and universities in their public service activities respond to financial realities and to social structure.

ORIENTATION

A special aspect of mission is that of orientation. A college or university may be residentially oriented or it may be urban oriented. There is another kind of orientation which we mentioned earlier: the orientation of church affiliation or the orientation of nonsectarian commitment. Although in a few instances "church relatedness" may be of some importance (for example, in student recruitment, staffing, or instructional emphasis), the religious orientation of higher education does not appear to be a major factor at the end of the twentieth century. The residential orientation versus an urban orientation does remain of vital importance in college or university mission.

The ideal location of the college or university of the nineteenth century in the United States was a small community removed from the distractions and temptations of the large city. Colleges and universities founded principally by the Young Men's Christian Association and by orders of the

Catholic Church were oriented toward urban youth. In a few instances, city governments, such as New York City, sought to redress the imbalance resulting from the location of so many state universities in small, distant communities. Among the 20 most populous states, in 18 instances the "flagship" state university was not located in the state's largest city as late as 1980.

The difference between a residential orientation and an urban orientation is not a matter of location. It is a matter of institutional commitment. There are colleges and universities located in large urban areas which are not oriented to the urban community of which they are a part. It is possible for a college or university to be *in* a city but not *of* the city. Other colleges and universities are both in a city and of the city.

The residential college or university undertakes as a major aspect of its mission to integrate classroom and other learning with full-time student residence in the academic community. The residential university may house a large proportion of the enrolled student body, or a considerable proportion of the student body may reside in the vicinity of the university in private housing. The residential university tends to operate as a self-contained community where students may be engaged in formal learning some 48 hours a week and where students may be residents of the academic community the remaining 120 hours a week.

The residential university is likely to be more expensive to operate than the urban university. This difference is clearly evident in the income and expenditure for so-called auxiliary enterprises. The residential university is likely to be more expensive for the student to attend, since the student must meet residential costs (including transportation) in addition to instructional charges. These residential costs include not only housing and food service but also many student activity and service costs, such as health service, recreational service, cultural service, and community service.

The university with an urban orientation serves primarily a commuting, a part-time, an employed, and often an older student body. These students carry on their learning activity within the environment of the urban university. They carry on their living activity within the environment of the urban community.

The essential differences between a residential university and an urban university lie in the content of learning and in the learning process. The mission of the residential university is primarily concerned with theoretical learning, which involves classroom discussion, laboratory experimentation, library reading, and peer group interaction. The mission of the urban university is to integrate learning and practical experience, learning and urban life. The mission of the urban university shares the learning process with workplace, family, and urban community.

The urban-oriented university is "place-bound." The urban university must, to the fullest extent possible and feasible, meet the needs of the student who lives and works in the urban community. Part-time students and employed students are not able to move to a residential university because of their work ties and living ties to the city where they reside. The urban university must, within reasonable limits, seek to meet the total learning needs of students who live and work in the urban area.

As they have approached the 1980s, some colleges and universities have sought to combine the residential mission with the urban mission. Such institutions are located in sizable urban communities but have in the past espoused a residential rather than an urban mission. It is doubtful that such colleges and universities have given careful attention to the basic learning differences between the residential institution and the urban institution. Whether or not any particular university can effectively combine the two missions remains to be demonstrated.

It has sometimes been claimed that the residential university is a "better university" than the urban university. Factually, the correct statement is that the residential university is different from the urban university. The two universities have a different mission, a different kind of student body, a different kind of learning process. Both kinds of universities are essential to the goals of higher education in American society.

ACCESS

From the point of view of a particular student, admission to college enrollment is a matter of student interest and student financing. From the point of view of a particular college or university, admission to enrollment is a matter of admission standards and of student competence. The college or university is also interested in the student's ability to meet the costs of enrollment, both in the interest of encouraging the enrollment of students of special or outstanding talent and in the interest of promoting educational justice. A student picks the college or university that he or she wishes to enter. The university picks the students that it wishes to enroll.

In essence, there are two forms of admission practiced by a college or university: (1) open admission and (2) selective admission. Open admission provides access for any high school graduate interested in enrolling, and for any non-high-school graduate presenting evidence of the equivalence of a secondary education. Community colleges, technical institutes, some urban universities, and some other colleges and universities do practice open access at the undergraduate level. Selective admission occurs when applications for enrollment exceed planned size, or when a minimum standard of competence is required for admission to an instructional program. Admission to many undergraduate programs in the applied arts and most graduate and professional programs (medicine, law, dentistry, optometry, veterinary medicine, and theology) are based on selective admission.

Open admission is the mechanism for universal access to higher education. But open admission does not imply the absence of standards of competence in an instructional program; open admission signifies only that a student has the opportunity to demonstrate, by classroom and other performance, his or her competence to meet prescribed standards. Any instructional program practicing open admission is likely to have a high attrition rate, because many students will not meet performance standards.

Open admission carries with it an obligation to assist students to meet expected standards of learning and skill. Open admissions requires extensive student services in counseling and in the development of learning skills. Without such remedial assistance, open admission becomes a revolving door whereby students enter and leave in a short span of time. Open admission is more expensive for a college or university than selective admission.

The basic problem in selective admission is simply that of the criteria to be used in determining those applicants to be permitted to enroll. There are various available criteria: rank in high school class or college class (such as top 15 percent or top 50 percent); percentile rank or imputed score on a standardized test; demonstrated performance skill; personal references; personal interview and responses to a personal questionnaire. In some circumstances legal residence may be a factor in student admissions: some state universities may admit only students who are residents of the state to an instructional program (such as law school or medical school), while some private colleges and universities may seek to enroll students from a region or even nationwide. In some instances, sons and daughters of alumni may be given some preference in admissions.

The objective in selective admissions is twofold: (1) to

admit the most highly qualified students (that is, those most likely to satisfactorily complete a degree program), and (2) to admit students who will in general exemplify a high standard of competence in professional practice after graduation. There are no certain and infallible indicators in student selection of those individuals who will complete a degree program and subsequently reflect credit upon the college or university. Over time, a college or university may use statistical analyses to find out which criteria correlate most closely with "successful" student achievement. But there is inevitably some element of judgment in selective admissions, and some element of failure. Selective admission endeavors to reduce to a minimum the element of failure.

For several years the standardized test has come under criticism as a criterion for selective admission. The primary criticism has been that tests tend to measure competence in responding to test questions rather than competence in pursuing a particular degree program. A secondary criticism has been that standardized tests are culturally biased, favoring the student whose social environment has provided an extensive opportunity to read and to acquire facts, while disadvantaging the student from an unfavorable social environment.

In the criticism of standardized testing two considerations are often overlooked. First, the standardized test was devised in order to permit individual comparisons of ability regardless of high school or college attended, regardless of place of residence, regardless of social circumstance. Second, the standardized test does tend to provide a forecast of competence to complete a degree program. Most admission officers and committees will seldom make decisions based solely upon a test score, but they usually find test scores one among several indicators helpful in arriving at a judgment about what applicants to admit to a degree program and what applicants to reject. In selective admission, some applicants fail to obtain admission.

The moral standard of educational justice has come in conflict with the practice of selective admission. Educational justice seeks to ensure that blacks, American Indians, Asian Americans, and individuals of Hispanic culture shall have equality of access to instructional programs along with whites of Anglo-Saxon and other European ethnic origin. The argument is that for social and cultural reasons—including a background of slavery, poverty, and cultural discrimination—members of certain minority groups cannot be judged by the same standards of competence applied to others. Educational justice in our society is not served by a single standard of meritocracy but must be served by variable standards which will ensure access for disadvantaged minorities. While racial or ethnic quotas in selective admission have been found by the Supreme Court to be unconstitutional, some "reasonable" form of preference for minority students has been upheld. Selective admission practices have had to find in some way these reasonable preferences in order to meet the standard of educational justice.

One final comment is needed. A single university may practice open admission for some instructional programs and selective admission for other instructional programs. Admission is often to programs rather than to a university as an enterprise, and so various standards of access may exist within a university.

No part of a statement of mission for a college or university is more important than the statement on standards of access. Colleges and universities can be and are distinctive in their standards of access. The least a college or university can do is to make those standards explicit. Over time the standards may change, becoming more or less selective, but the prevailing standard deserves to be known.

ENROLLMENT SIZE

As we have noted earlier, colleges and universities differ in their enrollment size. Some colleges and universities are small; others are large. Some are growing in enrollment, some are declining in enrollment, and some are remaining stable in enrollment. The mission of a college or university may be to expand, to contract, or to remain the same in size. The enrollment mission may reflect purposes of growth, or it may reflect response to an external environment that is causing a contraction in size and scope. A college or university may not have control over its enrollment. Moreover, program offerings, qualitative standards, and instructional orientation may affect enrollment trends. A college or university may desire growth but experience a decline. A college or university may desire stability in enrollment and may be able to achieve it. The mission of enrollment size is likely to reflect, or to be the consequence of, other missions. The mission of enrollment size is seldom self-fulfilling.

The mission of enrollment size has important implications for other missions. For example, a university may decide that it wishes to maintain a particular level of enrollment, or even to expand its enrollment. Such a university may then have to reexamine its instructional objectives, programs, and orientation; it may have to reexamine its mission in access, enrollment characteristics, and standards of quality. Another university may decide that it wishes to maintain existing instructional objectives, programs, and orientation; it may wish to maintain selective admission, current enrollment characteristics, and current standards of quality. The university may then have an enrollment mission that adjusts to these other missions.

It is also possible that because of a declining enrollment a college or university may wish to expand or enlarge its research mission and its public service mission. The limiting factors in this kind of mission readjustment are staff competence and financial resources. The importance of the enrollment mission is obvious. Size affects income, programs, and quality. Here again, many colleges and universities have tended not to be explicit about their enrollment mission, and have failed to give the matter the careful attention it deserves. This circumstance is likely to be all the more critical as higher education confronts a declining 18- to 22-year-old age group in society during the 1980s.

ENROLLMENT CHARACTERISTICS

Another distinctive aspect of a college or university lies in its enrollment characteristics. The residentially oriented college or university tends to enroll full-time students in the traditional age brackets for undergraduate students (18 to 22 years) and for graduate students (22 to 26 years). The urban-oriented college or university tends to enroll part-time rather than full-time students, commuting rather than residential students, older students rather than students of the traditional ages. These differences in student characteristics have their impact upon instructional programs and upon instructional practices.

Because of the personal cost involved, the undergraduate student of traditional college age enrolled in a residential university is likely to come from a relatively affluent family. This student is likely to be in a transitional phase from the constraints of family authority upon personal behavior to the constraints of a personally imposed standard of conduct. This student is likely to be concerned about social issues affecting persons of a more disadvantaged socioeconomic status. The intellectual, social, and emotional point of view of the residential undergraduate student is likely to be quite different from the point of view of the part-time, employed, and older student of the urban university.

Faculty members and administrative officers of a residential university located in a large city are likely to be pulled in different directions. On the one hand, they are committed to the learning process of a residential university. On the other hand, they cannot escape the evidences of urban degradation. The response may be a desire to "do something" for the city, without a careful assessment of just what that something might reasonably and feasibly be. Sometimes this response is a desire to enroll more students from the immediate urban community, when in fact the university is not prepared for or ready to assist students from a disadvantaged urban environment.

It must be emphasized that students from different socioeconomic backgrounds tend to have quite different characteristics, and quite different learning needs. It is not enough for a university to be concerned about the intellectual competence of the students it enrolls. It is equally important for the university to be concerned about the socioeconomic characteristics of the student it enrolls. These differences affect the learning process just as much as differences in intellectual abilities. As colleges and universities have enrolled students of more diverse socioeconomic characteristics, they may have been somewhat slow or even inept in adapting their learning procedures to a diverse student body.

A different circumstance is presented by the college or university with a predominantly black student enrollment. Just as many religious denominations established colleges and universities in the 1800s and early in the 1900s in order to ensure educational opportunity for young people of their particular faith, so black leaders after the Civil War began to build colleges and universities to provide opportunity for black youth. As of 1978, there were some 110 colleges and universities with a predominantly black student body. These colleges and universities functioned under both public and private sponsorship.

In many southern states after 1865, separate public colleges and universities were created for black students, while other state colleges and universities continued to serve an exclusively white student body. After the Brown case of 1954, and more particularly after the enactment of the Civil Rights Act of 1964 by the federal government, the discrimination against black students in all-white public colleges and universities began to come to an end. Private colleges and universities, which in general had never discriminated against black students, began to give increased attention to the enrollment of black students.

As of 1980, the public policy issue is whether or not there should continue to be colleges and universities with the mission of serving a predominantly black student body. The answer to this issue on the part of black leaders themselves is yes. The distinguished retired president of Morehouse College has written: "So, I for one will fight to maintain the black image in education and fight for the survival of black colleges. Integration must never mean the liquidation of black colleges." * Similarly, the president of the National Urban League has asserted: "The black institutions of higher education are a basic resource and institutional bulwark of the black community. Black colleges stand, not as remnants of segregation, but as positive community resources reflecting the needs and the identity of black Americans. There will always be a need for identifiably black institutions, just as there will always be a need for other religiously and ethnically based colleges and universities." †

* Benjamin E. Mays, "The Black College in Higher Education," in Charles V. Willie and Ronald R. Edmonds, eds., *Black Colleges in America* (New York: Teachers College Press, 1978), p. 27.
† Vernon E. Jordan, "How Far We Still Must Go," *AGB Reports*, July/August 1979, p. 11.

The issue is no longer whether or not black students should be admitted to colleges and universities with a predominantly white student body. This issue has already been settled, and black students are enrolled in both public and private colleges and universities which have a preponderance of white students. This is true in southern states as well as in other states. Black students who wish to enroll in colleges and universities with a preponderantly white student body and who have a reasonable prospect of meeting institutional standards of quality are now able to enroll.

The issue of the 1980s is whether or not the colleges and universities with a predominantly black enrollment should continue in existence. Black leaders in general say that they should continue to exist. Insofar as public colleges and universities are concerned, those serving a predominantly black student body must have the same comparable financial support as other public colleges and universities, and even something extra in order to meet the special needs of black students. In some instances, in particular in cities where there is one public university with a predominantly white student body and another public university with a predominantly black student body, civil rights leaders and federal courts have insisted upon a merger, or upon a non-duplicative distribution of instructional programs in order that each university will equally serve white and black students.

The difficulty with such mergers, or with such distribution of programs, is simply that the alternative of choice for the black student is then eliminated. If a black student believes that he or she is more likely to achieve instructional and personal development within a learning environment of predominantly white students, then this choice ought to be available. If a black student believes that he or she is more likely to achieve instructional and personal development within a learning environment of predominantly black students, then this choice ought to be available. Certainly such a choice seems appropriate for the undergraduate student, especially in undergraduate programs in the arts and sciences, business administration, and teacher education. Such a choice is less appropriate in graduate instruction or in first professional programs of instruction, where black and white students should be intermingled.

The mission of colleges and universities can be distinctive in terms of student characteristics, and student characteristics have their impact upon other missions and upon the performance of colleges and universities.

QUALITY

The quality of instructional performance, the quality of research and public service performance, and the quality of a college or university in general may vary substantially from one enterprise to another. Yet quality is an elusive attribute to define, let alone to measure or evaluate. Most persons in academic life acknowledge qualitative differences in the mission and performance of particular colleges and universities but have great difficulty in stating evidence of these differences.

It is customary to equate quality with inputs of the academic enterprise: the quality of student admissions measured by test scores and rank in class; the quality of the faculty (the proportion with Ph.D. degrees); the compensation paid faculty members and staff; the library resources and the presence of a computer on campus; the quality of the physical facilities (buildings and equipment); the predominance of full-time rather than part-time faculty members; the physical attraction of campus buildings and grounds; a low ratio of students to faculty members; a relatively modest instructional workload for faculty members (four or five courses in a two-semester academic year with enrollment of 20 or fewer students per course); a substantial research and public service budget; a high rate of instructional expenditures per student; and a high rate of support program expenditures per student.

Measurements of outputs are not nearly so precise as are the measurements of inputs. The number of degrees granted by each instructional program is well known, as is the attrition rate between entering students and graduating students. But the extent and scope of learning achieved by each graduate are not so easy to determine. Some baccalaureate students will take standardized admission tests for graduate and graduate professional schools, and the admissions achievements of these graduates supposedly reflects the quality of undergraduate learning accomplished. The placement record in jobs is another presumed indicator of learning. The eventual professional and other achievements of alumni are thought to indicate the quality of college or university performance.

There are other measurements available: scholarly books and articles published by faculty members; creative works of art executed or performed; consulting and other public service demands upon faculty time. Such outputs tell us something about the quality of research, creativity, and public service. Peer evaluation of faculty performance is another procedure for determining quality.

Some additional efforts are being made today through testing of all those completing an undergraduate program to suggest the quality of undergraduate instruction. It remains uncertain whether or not such testing will provide the desired measurements, and whether or not faculties will be willing to approve such testing.

The fact remains that in spite of all the known deficiencies in determining college or university quality, there are qualitative differences among academic enterprises. Some colleges and universities are perceived as being of high quality; some are perceived as being of medium quality; some are perceived as being of modest quality. Such perceptions are generalizations about the products (graduates, research, creative activity, public service, educational justice, constructive criticism) of particular academic enterprises. Individual graduates of a college or university of modest quality may become distinguished professional practitioners and public leaders.

Colleges and universities are often reluctant to acknowledge that they have distinctive missions in terms of quality. Yet there is a need and a utility in having colleges and universities of different quality. Indeed, if we had adequate measurements we might find that universities of open admission or of modest admission standards achieve more learning for a graduate than universities of higher selectivity in the admission of students.

America is well served by diversity in the qualitative standards of various colleges and universities, even though the colleges and universities are reluctant to admit their distinctive qualitative differences. There has been a need for professional practitioners and for social leaders of varied abilities, and American higher education has provided graduates of varied competencies.

RESOURCES

Finally, we must emphasize that there are distinctive income and capital resources available to colleges and universities. State governments may endeavor to equalize the support provided public colleges and universities, and to a substantial degree such equity has been achieved in state appropriation processes. But public colleges and universities differ in the non-state government support they obtain, and these differences are to be commended rather than criticized. Some private colleges and universities have generous endowments and others have meager or almost no endowment. Some private colleges and universities obtain generous support from alumni, church bodies, and other individuals and groups;

others receive only modest philanthropic support. Colleges and universities with large enrollments tend to experience economies of scale unavailable to colleges and universities of small enrollment.

The problem for colleges and universities is to match their instructional, research, public service, access, enrollment, and qualitative missions with their financial resources. A college or university must ever be concerned that its resource mission—its resource prospects—keep pace with all other aspects of its mission. There is no end to the financial needs of a college or university, but there are definite limits to the financial resources of a college or university in any given time period.

Many colleges and universities have champagne appetites and beer incomes. It is never simple to reduce appetites to income, aspirations to financial realities. The mission of a college or university must eventually be determined by resources.

CONCLUSION

The statement of mission of a college or university is a statement of purposes to which the particular enterprise is committed, and for which it has the necessary resources. Organizational structure, program objectives, and program performance are governed by mission.

Colleges and universities cannot escape the challenge of mission. The more specific, the more precise, the more realistic the mission of an academic enterprise, the more effective will be the organizational structure in encouraging the accomplishment of that mission. Much of the conflicts within colleges and universities about management, governance, and leadership are in fact conflicts about mission. If the mission of a college or university can be stated and agreed to with some degree of general commitment, organizational structure will begin to be understood in its proper perspective.

4

Management Structure of the University

Because colleges and universities are productive enterprises, it is appropriate to emphasize management over governance and leadership. It is by its management performance that a college or university is necessarily judged. Leadership may inspire management, and governance may support management. It is by the effectiveness of its work planning and work performance that a college or a university accomplishes its missions.

Perhaps no aspect of a college or university is more frequently overlooked, or more frequently misunderstood, than its management. Higher education enterprises seek dynamic, decisive leadership. Higher education enterprises continually discuss their structure and process of governance. These same enterprises tend to ignore their structure and process of man-

MANAGEMENT STRUCTURE OF THE UNIVERSITY

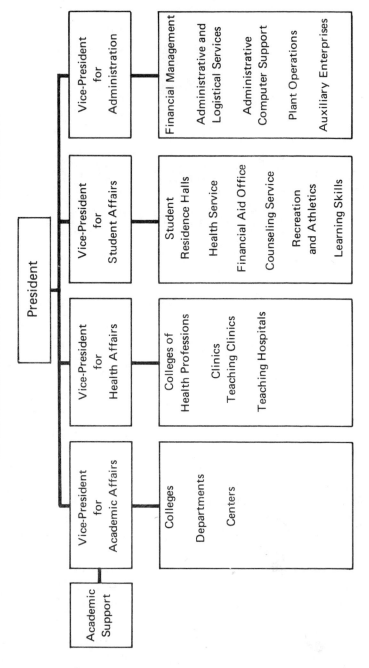

agement. Yet it is the structure and process of management which are of primary importance to effective and efficient performance. It is the structure and process of management which produce the outputs the enterprise exists to accomplish.

There are probably two or three reasons why management structure and process receive so little attention and discussion in higher education discourse. Management is a word more commonly associated with business enterprises and government enterprises than with higher education enterprises. Some faculty members resent any implication that the learning process can be "managed," or that faculty members are to be managed. Management connotes a structure and process that appears alien to the faculty mind.

This suspicion, even hostility, is reinforced by the failure of faculty members to understand that they are in fact the managers of the higher education enterprise. To the extent that the learning process is "managed," faculty members, not deans or vice-presidents or presidents, are the managers. Faculty members are professional practitioners, practitioners of the scholar/teacher profession or of the scholar/researcher profession. Faculty members practice their profession within a particular learning environment which is labeled a college or university. Faculty members do not charge their students directly for the professional service rendered. But faculty members are nonetheless professional practitioners of scholarship. The individual faculty member manages his or her professional practice. No plan or blueprint of the enterprise can do more than suggest or outline the desired product. The faculty member individually produces learning.

Much depends upon how one defines management in the context of the academic enterprise. I employ a simple definition of management as a process. Management is work planning and work performance. Management is determining work objectives, work technology, and necessary work resources. Management is the production of work outputs with the planned technology and the planned resources. And management is the evaluation of the quality of the work output.

It is necessary to state again the work outputs of the academic enterprise: student instruction accomplished, research undertaken and completed, creative activity realized, public service performed, educational justice achieved, constructive criticism explained. These outputs result from the learning process, which only faculty members can manage, which only faculty work planning and work performance can accomplish. The management of the outputs of the academic enterprise is not just vested in faculty members; it is inherent in the very concept of being a faculty member, of being a scholar.

For some erroneous reason, management within the academic enterprise is equated with the work undertaken by the support programs. The librarian is a manager, the university doctor is a manager, the university personnel director is a manager, the university comptroller is a manager, the university superintendent of buildings and grounds is a manager. To be sure, all such individuals are managers. But they are managers of *support* programs; they provide services essential to the operation of the academic enterprise. They are not managers of the outputs of the academic enterprise; they are assistants to such managers. The management of support programs is indispensable to the management of output programs. The two kinds of programs should never be confused, and the priority of output over support ought never to be doubted.

There is another factor in the misunderstanding about the managerial status and role of the faculty member. The managerial structure and process in the production of the outputs of the academic enterprise are highly decentralized. We shall say more about this characteristic of organization in a moment. The managerial structure and process for the performance of support programs tend to be highly centralized within an academic enterprise. There are good and sufficient reasons for both arrangements. But this organizational difference is no justificarion for failing to understand the managerial role of the faculty member, or for failing to emphasize the management authority and responsibility of the faculty member.

The traditional organization chart of a university may be one reason that management as a structure and process is misunderstood in an academic enterprise. Such a traditional organization chart is shown at the beginning of this chapter. It has the fault of all organization charts; it conceals as much as it reveals, it confuses as well as advances understanding. One may inquire why we should employ organization charts anyway. The response is that such charts are a useful introduction to understanding. Such charts must never be considered as the end of understanding.

And in these introductory observations some comment must be made about faculty collective bargaining. If faculty members are managers of learning, why should managers seek to bargain collectively? If faculty members are supposed to bargain with management, who and what is this management which faculty members bargain with? Neither question is simple to answer, and both questions represent illustrations of the failure to appreciate the management structure and process of the academic enterprise.

Faculty members resort to collective bargaining because of dissatisfaction essentially with the governance structure and process of the academic enterprise. Faculty members bargain collectively with the governance structure of the enterprise: the governing board and the president as professional adviser to the governing board. Faculty members resort to collective bargaining because they are dissatisfied with their economic remuneration within the enterprise and are anxiety-prone about a threatening future for the academic enterprise.

ACADEMIC AFFAIRS

The basic work unit of an instructional department is a course. Students register for a course; a faculty member instructs students in a course. A course consists of instructional objectives, an instructional process or technology, and an evaluation of student learning accomplished. The course completed satisfactorily by the student becomes one part of the total requirements for award of a degree.

Faculty members are ordinarily grouped into instructional departments that coincide with particular disciplines of the arts and sciences and particular specializations in technical education and in professional education. The department is usually presided over by an executive officer who is a kind of *primus inter pares*, a first among equals. While courses are likely to reflect the special interest and competence of an individual faculty member, a department brings together a group of persons of related interests and competencies.

The department is concerned primarily with relationships among faculty members professing a common discipline or a common specialization. Course offerings are usually planned by departments with some element of coherence and some element of sequence: introductory, basic, and specialized.

Departments are grouped together in colleges or schools. The familiar groupings are as follows:

Technologies
 Business and commerce
 Data processing
 Health services
 Mechanical and engineering
 Natural sciences
 Public service

Arts and Sciences
  Area studies
  Biological sciences
  Humanities and foreign languages
  Physical sciences and mathematics
  Social and behavioral sciences
  Interdisciplinary studies
Professional Fields
  Agriculture and natural resources
  Architecture and environmental design
  Business and management
  Communications
  Computer and information services
  Education
  Engineering
  Fine and applied arts
  Health professions
  Home economics
  Library science
  Nursing
  Pharmacy
  Physical education and recreation
  Public affairs
  Social work
First (or Graduate) Professional
  Dentistry
  Law
  Medicine
  Optometry
  Osteopathic medicine
  Theology
  Veterinary medicine

There are several well-known disciplines or specializations in the arts and sciences which are not included in this outline. Thus, the humanities include English language and literature, comparative literature, philosophy, religious studies, speech and drama, and sometimes history, in addition to classics and modern foreign languages. The social sciences include anthropology, economics, geography, history, government, social psychology, statistics, and sociology. Within these disciplines are a considerable array of further specialization (such as in government between American political institutions, comparative political institutions, international relations and law, and political theory). Within the sub-specializations are yet further specializations (such as in American political institutions between federal government, state and local government, constitutional law, political parties and behavior, and public administration). Scholarly competence in higher education tends to be equated with specialization.

On occasion, interdisciplinary studies may be offered. Thus, a specialization in American Studies may involve a combination of courses in American literature, American history, American government, and American sociology. Similar interdisciplinary programs and area study programs may be developed to meet some instructional objectives.

The various groupings of disciplines and professional fields of study just listed also involve *levels* of specialization. The technologies are usually programs of two years' duration eventuating in an associate degree (usually the associate in applied science). The disciplines of the arts and sciences involve three levels of specialization: bachelor's, master's, and doctor's. Most professional fields of study also involve the same three levels of specialization, although some fields tend to be graduate level (master's and doctor's) only, as in library science, public affairs, and social work. The first professional or graduate professional fields of study usually require a baccalaureate as a prerequisite for admission.

The term "instructional program" represents both a subject or field of specialization and a level of specialization, represented by award of a degree (associate, bachelor's, master's, and doctor's). The graduate professional fields have their own particular degrees such as Juris Doctor (for law), Doctor of Medicine, and Doctor of Veterinary Medicine. Instructional programs are the specialized "concentrations" which a college or university decides are appropriate to its mission, meet a student interest, fulfill a social need (professional employment), and can generate income consistent with expenditure requirements.

There is an additional kind of instructional program which, for lack of a better term, we ordinarily label "general education." We have referred briefly to the complexities of this endeavor in the preceding chapter. It is necessary here only to mention that general education as usually conceived and practiced has two instructional objectives in mind: (1) the non-professional, non-employment-oriented instruction of students (education for its own sake or education for "life" rather than education for a "living") and (2) the provision of a knowledge base for professional application. A useful illustration of this second kind of objective is provided by the traditional pattern of medical education, which is divided into two years of "basic" science (anatomy, biochemistry, microbiology, physiology, biophysics, pharmacology) and two years of clinical science (obstetrics and gynecology, pediatrics, internal medicine, surgery, and psychiatry).

In instructional planning it is not too difficult to convince students of the need to acquire the knowledge base relevant to professional practice, although how best to integrate theory with practice, or knowledge with application, remains an instructional complexity. It is more difficult to convince students of an intrinsic value in the knowledge of the disciplines as a means of understanding and appreciating the "humane" life. American students tend to expect a utilitarian or instrumental value to be achieved through higher education rather than an intrinsic value. The expectation arises from the very nature of American civilization as it has developed since 1607.

Instructional programs are essentially the specializations offered by departments, and occasionally by a school or college. Thus a school of nursing, a college of law, and others may not have departmental specialization even though they have other specialization.

There are two peculiarities of program structure which may be imposed upon departments and colleges from an all-university point of view. One peculiarity is the general education program with a set of course requirements expected to be met by all students regardless of their special interest. A second peculiarity of program organization is the graduate school, an artificial construct intended to give special attention to the management performance of those departments authorized to offer programs for the master's degree and the doctoral degree.

Instructional management is concerned to produce student learning. If faculty members—if anyone—knew more about the psychology of learning, perhaps instructional management would be more effective, more certain of actually producing student learning. In the absence of more than some tentative ideas about learning as a matter of content and of process, faculty members can do no more than practice their craft to the best of their individual ability.

Just as the faculty member is hampered in his or her productive efforts by a limited knowledge of learning, so also is the student similarly hampered. Presumably the student by his or her presence in a college or university has indicated an interest in learning. While this assumption may be valid in most instances, in some cases the student may be simply marking time for lack of something better to do. There are probably as many different reasons for wanting to learn a particular field of study as there are individual students in a college or university. We know certain generalizations about student motivation: intellectual curiosity, interest and skill in a particular kind of learning, desire to "get ahead" socially and economically, family expectation. How these motivations separately and in combination encourage and assist student learning, we know only vaguely. Again, we know little about the physiology and psychology of learning from the point of view of the student participant. Medical science tells us that learning and memory are two of the remarkable aspects of the human brain. But how the brain of the student achieves and stores learning remains essentially a mystery. We know that people do learn and do remember, and we know that these competencies are unevenly rather than evenly distributed among the human species.

In the learning process—in the interaction of scholar/ teacher and of student—the emphasis in college or university is upon content rather than upon procedure. Faculty members are first of all specialists in an area or field of knowledge or of cultural performance; only secondarily is the scholar/ teacher a competent communicator or transmitter of knowledge or of cultural skill. Academic management is continually complicated by this faculty characteristic of content specialization and of a lesser competence in the communication process.

Instructional management is first of all concerned with learning programs. But instructional management is also concerned with instructional resources: faculty personnel, classroom and laboratory facilities, and learning resources. A great deal of faculty attention in departments and in larger groupings of a division, school, or college is necessarily devoted to instructional resources: to faculty personnel actions (recruitment, promotion, tenure, development, and compensation), to planning the construction and remodeling of facilities, and to the acquisition and use of learning resources. Faculty members as a departmental grouping and as representatives of larger entities (a college) are likely to spend more time planning and carrying out this concern with resources than in planning and carrying out their concern with learning.

It must be emphasized that instruction of students is only one part of academic management. The faculty member as scholar/teacher or as artist/teacher must also be involved in advancing his or her own learning. The external public is likely to believe that once a faculty member acquires the competence to instruct students, that competence is ever present and unchanging. The fact is otherwise. The scholar/teacher or the artist/teacher never ceases in his or her own efforts to learn or to perfect a performing skill. Scholarship must be kept up to date, must explore new possibilities or probabilities of knowledge. The artist/teacher can retain a performance skill only by constant practice.

It is easy to label some of these efforts to advance scholarship as research, or some of these efforts to advance performance skill as creative activity. But only some scholar/teachers become scholar/researchers in a formal sense of contributing to the advancement of knowledge. Few scholar/teachers and few artist/teachers become creative artists in the sense of achieving distinction as a writer, performer, or artist. Yet all scholar/teachers and all artist/teachers must develop their scholarly or their artistic competencies continually. The limited time of a scholar/teacher or of an artist/teacher devoted to student instruction per full-time work week is an acknowledgment of this continuing effort of the teacher to improve his or her own competence as a scholar or as an artist. There are of course some scholar/teachers who do not maintain their scholarly competence; there are some artist/teachers who do not maintain their artistic competence. The failure of college or university learning management has usually been one of personnel management: a failure to evaluate faculty development and to discontinue the employment of faculty members whose continuing professional competence is not maintained.

Apart from the scholar/teacher's endeavors to maintain professional competence, some part of the work effort of the individual faculty member may be devoted to formal research and formal creative activity. Sometimes research or creative activity is not recognized as a departmental productive output, the way student instruction is. The one academic unit where this recognition does occur is the college or school of medicine. Perhaps this circumstance results from the extensive external funding available for research in the health sciences. Otherwise, only departments in large research universities tend to manage research even as they manage student instruction.

Public service is yet another output of departments. Because of the existence of the cooperative extension service, faculty members in colleges of agriculture are often heavily involved in public service. And because of the existence of teaching hospitals, faculty members in colleges of medicine are often heavily involved in public service. On occasion, other departments or colleges have organized public service activities, such as a telecommunications center, a materials testing laboratory, a speech and hearing clinic, an animal hospital, an educational services bureau, a legal aid center, a survey research center (which is a public service, not a research activity), a testing service, a computer applications service, and a market research center.

To some extent faculty members may engage in research and public service activities "off campus," either on an individual basis or on an organized basis. A management issue must then be resolved; namely, determining the extent to which such external activity is consistent with full-time service as a faculty member. One response, perhaps the prevailing response, by colleges and universities is to set a policy that full-time faculty service requires the minimum presence of a faculty member on campus four days a week, seven hours a day.

Thus far in this discussion of the management of academic affairs we have focused attention on academic departments. As we have indicated, sometimes academic departments are grouped into divisions; more frequently they are grouped into schools or colleges with a director or dean as an academic manager. The role of a dean in a professional college is apt to be somewhat more vital in academic management than the role of a dean of a college of arts and sciences. The role again has elements of work planning and performance and of resource management.

It has been said with some justification that in a university the dean occupies the "last" or "highest" position where there is any actual opportunity to influence work production: planning, performance, and resources for learning, research, creative activity, and public service. The dean is an instigator of planning, a promoter of new endeavors, a supervisor of outputs, an evaluator of outcomes, a reviewer of departmental personnel actions, a claimant for the financial and other resources of the university. The dean is an academic planner, an academic manager, an academic personnel officer, and an academic budget officer one step removed from the operational level of the academic department.

Sometimes a university makes budget allocations to a dean rather than to a department for faculty clerical support, faculty travel, instructional supplies and equipment, and faculty development. Sometimes a dean supervises a research center or a public service program when these endeavors are attached to a college rather than to a department. Sometimes, when a college is large in faculty staffing and student enrollment, or highly specialized in its academic endeavor, academic support services (such as a specialized law library) or student support services (such as placement and student financial aid) may be decentralized to the level of a dean's management authority.

Within the academic structure of a university, the vice-president for academic affairs is the institution-wide manager. The vice-president for academic affairs must necessarily evidence a university-wide point of view on academic affairs. There is a major limitation inherent in this position, since a university-wide point of view on instructional issues is likely to be negligible. At the same time, the vice-president is a managing supervisor of certain important academic support services.

A word is necessary here about these academic support services. The standard chart of accounts recommended by the National Association of College and University Business Officers classifies student admissions and records as "student services." I feel strongly that these are misclassified; an office of student admissions and a Registrar's Office are closely related to the conduct of instructional programs. These offices manage basic academic policies involving standards of admission, course scheduling, grade records, and the fulfillment of degree requirements. These matters belong properly in the academic domain of university organization, and should properly be classified as academic support services managed on a university-wide basis and functioning under the supervision of the vice-president for academic affairs.

In addition, other academic support services on a university-wide basis include the library service, a computer service for instructional use, other learning resource services (such as an audio-visual service and a telecommunications service), and university-wide museums and galleries. These services are supervised by the vice-president for academic affairs.

On instructional/research/public service operations—the output part of academic affairs—the university-wide point of view is usually restricted to the development and supervision of broad general policies applicable to all output programs. In student instruction these policies may involve an all-university program of general studies as a component part of every undergraduate degree program, and certain standards in terms of length, quality, and cost of all degree programs. In research matters some policies and review procedure may be necessary at the vice-presidential level to ensure that these programs meet university standards, especially insofar as costs are concerned. The same process may be desirable for public service programs.

The vice-president's role is likely to be most demanding on budget and personnel matters. Shall faculty salaries be generally comparable among all instructional colleges and departments? Shall high-cost programs be undertaken? To what extent are university-wide standards of faculty workload desirable? How shall faculty workload be distributed in terms of cost and income between student instruction, research, and public service? What is the desirable relationship between faculty compensation and departmental support costs at the departmental level? These kinds of budget questions are troublesome, never fully resolved, and subject to continuing scrutiny.

On the personnel side there are questions of appointment standards and procedure, tenure standards and procedure, promotion standards and procedure, standards of faculty behavior, faculty evaluation standards and procedure, faculty development policies and practices (including sabbatical leaves), and termination standards and procedure. Like the academic budget, faculty personnel matters are always troublesome, never fully resolved, and subject to continuing scrutiny.

Today the tasks of the vice-president for academic affairs are so extensive and so demanding that one person cannot hope to carry the entire workload. While there is an organizational, and cost, danger in building a sizable bureaucracy at the vice-presidential level, some assistance must be provided. In a large university the vice-president may need an assistant vice-president for planning and budget, an assistant vice-president for personnel, an associate vice-president for undergraduate programs, and an associate vice-president for graduate studies and research (who might also be designated as dean of the graduate school).

Two other organizational observations must be addressed here. One observation has to do with the highly decentralized nature of the structure for performance of student instruction, research, and public service. The other observation has to do with faculty participation in management performance at the level of the dean of a college and at the level of a vice-president for academic affairs.

This discussion must emphasize the "bottom-up" nature of management in the academic enterprise. The impulse of management is not "top-down," as may be the case in a manufacturing enterprise, or even in a retail distribution enterprise. The individual faculty member and the separate academic department are not just the basic management units of student instruction, research, and public service; they are the location of management decision processes that determine the quality of instructional, research, and public service outcomes. Product planning and product performance is primarily a responsibility of the individual faculty member, reinforced by the faculty member's place in the academic department.

The role of a dean and a vice-president for academic affairs is essentially supportive of the faculty member's and the departmental performance in management. On rare occasion, when departmental management has been judged to be badly deficient in terms of university-wide standards, departmental decision making may be superseded. I know of one instance in a leading research university where a vice-president and a dean decided that a particular department was of very low quality in student instruction and research. The two officers constituted themselves a committee, along with one faculty member from another department, to undertake the recruitment of several new faculty members to be imposed upon the unsatisfactory department. As soon as a majority of professional positions had been filled with new recruits, management authority was returned to the individual faculty members and the department. This procedure was unusual, but aroused no faculty controversy in the university because the objective was acceptable to faculty members generally (other than those in the department involved), and because the poor performance of the department was generally recognized.

In the 1980s the problems for deans and vice-presidents will center not so much on low-quality performance as on low student enrollment and on high cost of operation. The objective in management will obviously be to increase enrollment and to expand outputs *and income* in research and public service, or to reduce personnel resources and costs to a level consistent with work load. Here is a management challenge indeed!

The faculty role in management at the college level and the vice-presidential level is often confused. Faculty members and administrative officers fail to differentiate their management role from their governance role. A major thesis of this discussion is that the two roles are different. We shall explore this difference further in Chapter 6, "Governance of the University." Here it is relevant to observe that there is a faculty role in management at the dean's level and at the vice-presidential level, but that this role should be focused upon management issues.

I think it is desirable for the dean of a college and for a vice-president for academic affairs to have two faculty committees to work with them on management matters. I would designate one of these committees as a Planning Committee and the other as an Advisory Committee. The planning committee members and the advisory committee members at the dean's level should be composed of one person elected from each department. The committees at the vice-presidential level should be composed of one person elected from each college. A two- or three-year term of office would be desirable on these committees.

The planning committee should serve as adviser to the dean or to the vice-president on program planning and program budget issues. The advisory committee would serve as adviser on specific personnel actions as recommended by department chairmen or by deans. To be sure, I would expect deans to include department chairmen in both planning and personnel matters, and I would expect vice-presidents to meet frequently with a council of deans. But it is highly desirable to have a separate arrangement within colleges and within a university for faculty representation in management decision making. Such representation underlines the individual faculty role in academic management.

The management of academic affairs may appear from this description to be somewhat cumbersome. It is, however, a management structure that fits the realities of the learning process, as well as the realities of research and public service. It is a management structure that fits the professional role of faculty members. It is a management structure which clearly differentiates the academic enterprise from other productive enterprises.

HEALTH AFFAIRS

In those universities with colleges of medicine and with associated units in the health professions (such as a college of dentistry, a college of optometry, a school of nursing, a school of public health, a school of hospital administration, and a school of allied health professions), it has been found convenient, even essential, to organize health affairs under a vice-president separate from the vice-president for academic affairs. Instruction, research, and public service in the health science professions are sufficiently different and sufficiently complicated to justify a separate organizational structure. The differences are essentially differences of scale: the magnitude of the research effort and the magnitude of the public service effort in health care delivery to patients. Differences in scale are reflected in differences in the cost/income circumstances of health affairs.

We shall not undertake here to discuss student learning in medicine and other health professions, health science research, and health care delivery. In broad outline the concerns of health affairs are similar to the concerns of academic affairs already outlined. In details the differences are considerable. Controversy is just as prevalent in health affairs—I am tempted to say even more prevalent in health affairs—as in other academic affairs.

Colleges of medicine are highly selective in student admissions, and demand for such admission is substantially larger than the supply of enrollment opportunity. Because admission is thus tightly controlled to a prestigious and quite remunerative profession, there is a good deal of controversy about the standards and procedures of student selection. There is conflict about instructional objectives: the education of highly specialized medical practitioners, the education of general (family) medical practitioners, and the education of health science researchers. There is conflict about the allocation of income resources among student instruction, research, and health care delivery. There is conflict about the source and magnitude of total university income resources to be devoted to health affairs. There is conflict about who shall pay for health care delivery (patients, health insurance carriers, or governments) and there is conflict about who shall receive health care income (doctors or the university). There is conflict about health care delivery by a health science center in relation to private health care practitioners and government and voluntary hospitals. There is conflict about the obligations of a university health science center to health care delivery in a community, in a state, and in the nation. There is conflict about the relative roles of different professions (doctors, dentists, optometrists, osteopathic doctors, and nurses) in health care delivery. The university bold and brave enough to become involved in health affairs finds quickly enough that a president or a vice-president for academic affairs can't begin to find the time to worry about the conflicts in health affairs. The organizational response is to create the position of vice-president for health affairs. That response is no guarantee that the conflicts won't spill over onto the agenda of the university president. The organizational arrangement simply provides a structure for management direction which may be successful in resolving some of the issues, and in sharpening the definition of other issues requiring presidential attention and governance action.

STUDENT AFFAIRS

By way of contrast with academic affairs, student services are organized usually on a highly centralized basis. A vice-president for student affairs is a manager of various services which students may wish to make use of, or need to make use of, during their period of enrollment. It has been said that faculty members are concerned with students as learners, while student service officers are concerned with students as individuals or persons. The distinction has merit. Certainly on a residential campus the needs of students as persons are considerable. It is sometimes overlooked that on a residential campus an undergraduate student may devote as much as 45 or 48 hours per week to the formalized process of learning (classroom attendance, laboratory work, and reading) and the remaining 120 hours per week to other activities. The residential campus in varying ways becomes a self-contained community.

The residential campus usually supplies housing and food service for students, and a recreation and athletic service for students. The residential campus usually supplies cultural opportunities (music, theater, lectures, and art galleries), social opportunities (gathering places, social groupings, and social events), and community opportunities (a newspaper, broadcasting, community activities). To some extent similar services are made available to the commuting student.

Financial assistance has become a major student service on almost all campuses. Obviously higher education enrollment entails financial cost to students and their families: tuition and fee costs, residence costs, food costs, recreational and personal costs, and transportation costs. The charges to students vary, depending upon the extent of government and philanthropic subsidy, but these charges in some amount cannot be escaped by the individual student. Coming as they do from families of varied financial circumstances, students differ in the financial resources available to them with which to meet the personal costs of enrollment. Financial assistance endeavors to equalize somewhat the income resources of students.

Financial assistance serves an additional purpose: to recognize and reward learning achievement. Regardless of family economic circumstances, students of high academic accomplishment and potential, students of high artistic promise, and students of high athletic skill are in short supply. Many colleges and universities actively seek such students, and in competition with each other offer financial inducements to encourage enrollment at a particular campus. Such financial inducements are essential if a campus is to meet desired standards of student quality in its instructional and athletic programs.

Government programs of student financial assistance,

both federal and state, tend largely to achieve some degree of economic equality in student access to higher education en-rollment. Institutional programs from philanthropic sources and general income often tend largely to achieve quality in student access to higher education enrollment. Both purposes are appropriate.

Financial assistance to students involves grants, scholar-ships, fellowships (graduate), loans, prizes, and awards. In some instances the role of financial assistance management is to determine the recipients and the amount of the assistance, and to disburse the funds. In some instances the role of finan-cial assistance management is to assist students in obtaining available financing and to certify the eligibility of students for available financing. In loan management there is the further task of collecting payments of interest and principal. All of these tasks require careful and competent management. Some academic enterprises have failed to give this particular service the management competence it must necessarily have.

Many students seek employment in order to help meet personal costs. In fact, most student financial assistance programs require students to earn part of the income needed for higher education enrollment. Colleges and universities themselves employ numbers of students on a part-time basis, both to meet their employment needs (clerical, maintenance, food service, and other) and to assist students. Some instruc-tional programs operate on a cooperative basis, alternating periods of learning with periods of work experience. An employment office and a cooperative placement office then become necessary student services. In general, I believe that career placement should be an academic activity (as is stu-dent academic advising) rather than a student service.

Apart from finances, students have other problems: uncer-tainties about career interests, emotional difficulties, reli-gious uncertainties, complications in their sexual lives. Colleges and universities have found it useful to provide a counseling service to assist students in handling these aspects of their personal behavior. An additional student problem is a deficiency in learning skills, especially in reading, writing, and mathematical skills. Students who are deficient in these skills are unlikely to be able to complete a degree program of instruction. As a consequence, colleges and universities have had to organize a student development service, or a learning skills service. This is an essential student service, particularly as an indispensable corollary to an open admission policy.

It is apparent from this brief account that the provision of student services is an extensive endeavor. Moreover, the cost and the financing of these services have become troublesome issues. Shall students be taxed to support some services through a student activity and service fee? Shall students pay directly for services by means of prices based upon full cost? To what extent can and should government, philanthropic, and general income be used to support some of these services? These questions present issues to be resolved through the governance structure and process, but the management planning preceding governance actions begins with the student services management, and the effective and efficient performance of governance decisions on these issues must be achieved by the student service officers.

ADMINISTRATIVE SERVICES

Finally, another set of centralized support services usually operate under the supervision of a vice-president for administration, who sometimes is designated as the vice-president for finance and business, or simply as the chief "business" officer. These services include financial management (a bursar's office, an accounting office, a payroll office, an investment office, an internal audit office, and a property office), administrative and logistical services (purchasing, storage and distribution, nonacademic personnel, central printing and reproduction, communication service, and transportation service), a computer center (which may serve both instructional and administrative needs), plant operations service (including utilities and security service), and the management of auxiliary enterprises (including student residence halls, food service, bookstores, other housing facilities, and social and recreational facilities).

It is not necessary here to consider these services other than to enumerate their scope and to emphasize their importance. No campus can operate without these administrative services, and the cost of these services, especially of utility service, has become a matter of increasing concern. On the one hand, these services are indispensable to the operation of a campus; on the other hand, they are an overhead cost which must become a charge against output production. There is often an expectation among faculty members and students that administrative services should be more effectively or efficiently performed, and there may be some faculty and student dismay when it is realized that administrative services cost money.

One or two organizational concerns should be mentioned in connection with administrative services. First, both a vice-president for student affairs and a vice-president for administration are involved in the management of student housing, student food service, and student social and recreational facilities. The usual organizational distinction is one between "program management," which is a student affairs function, and "operational management," which is an administrative services function. Thus, the assignment of students to particular rooms and roommates in the residence halls and supervision of student life in the residence halls are student services. The housekeeping and maintenance of residence halls are administrative services. The social and recreational programs within a student center or a university center are student services; the operation of the physical facility or facilities for these services is an administrative service. Needless to say, a high degree of mutual understanding and cooperation is essential between the student services staff and the administrative services staff.

Second, we should note the appropriate definition of auxiliary enterprises. These enterprises have one characteristic in common: the costs (direct and indirect) are met by the prices charged to students or other customers. If a service is supported by prices rather than by the allocation of general or restricted income of the campus, then the service should be classified as an auxiliary enterprise and managed as an administrative service. If a service is supported by the allocation of general or restricted income of a campus, then the service should be classified as a student service and managed under the supervision of the vice-president for student affairs.

The case of intercollegiate athletics presents a particular problem, especially in the light of Title IX of the Higher Education Act of 1965, as amended. Title IX requires an equalization of programs and expenditures for recreational services and for intercollegiate athletics between men and women. In the past, intercollegiate athletics has been primarily a program of competition for men in "major" sports (football, basketball, baseball, track, and cross country) and in various minor sports (such as swimming, tennis, golf, soccer, and hockey). For certain universities, football and basketball have produced substantial income from ticket sales. Other intercollegiate sports were then supported by the "surplus" earnings from football and basketball and from general income.

It is obvious that Title IX forbids intercollegiate athletic competition for men and intercollegiate athletic competition for women. The problem then has become one of an appropriate balance, and a problem of cost and available income. It may be appropriate under these circumstances to restrict the definition of intercollegiate athletics as an auxiliary enterprise to those sports which produce substantial gate receipts. All other intercollegiate athletics might then be classified as a recreation and athletic service under the supervision of the vice-president for student affairs.

Administrative services must be managed, and must be managed well. Moreover, professional competence in the management of these services has increased substantially over the years, thanks in large part to the exemplary efforts of the National Association of College and University Business Officers. The business management of a college or university can never be taken for granted.

THE ADMINISTRATIVE ROLE OF THE PRESIDENT

Any description of the management structure of a college or university is incomplete without mention of the president. The president of a campus is its chief executive officer, and as such the president is manager-in-chief in addition to all other roles.

The managerial role of the president is one of exercising appropriate oversight to ensure that academic affairs, health affairs, student affairs, and administration are performed effectively and efficiently. The president cannot manage a college or university. But a president is expected to see to it that a college or university is well managed.

We shall observe later that the president of a college or university in his or her leadership role provides the necessary linkage between management and governance. This linkage is the means whereby management operations—both those of output programs and those of support programs—are joined to the decision-making structure and process, and the means whereby action is taken on purposes, policies, programs, and resources. As manager-in-chief, the president seeks to link management with governance, performance with decision. The intricacies of college or university governance necessarily have their impact upon college or university management. The complexities of college or university management necessarily have their impact upon college or university governance. The role of presidential leadership is to provide the bridge between management and governance.

CONCLUSION

Management is planning the productive operations of a college or university and presenting the essentials of such planning for approval or modification by the governance structure and process. Management is performing the productive operations of a college or university in order to effect governance decisions, and in order to accomplish planned outputs effectively and efficiently.

Management is also planning and performing support programs.

The management structure for academic affairs involving student instruction, research, and public service tends to be highly decentralized. The management structure for health affairs is similar in general outline to that for academic affairs. This management structure accomplishes the educational purposes, the output programs, of a college or university.

The management structure for student affairs and administrative services tends to be highly centralized. This management structure accomplishes the indispensable support needs, the support programs, of a college or university.

Management is a college or university at work.

5

Management
Process of
the University

Although our primary concern in this discussion is with the organizational structure of the university, the management tasks are so critical that some attention to the management processes of the university is warranted here. The fact will bear repetition: the university is a productive enterprise and management is the essence of productive endeavor. It is worthwhile to give note to the important considerations involved in the management performance of higher education outputs.

I have stressed already that management entails work planning and work performance. For our purposes in this chapter, I shall enlarge the definition somewhat in order to emphasize four basic components of the management process: (1) work planning, (2) work performance, (3) work re-

MANAGEMENT PROCESS OF THE UNIVERSITY

Work Planning	Work Performance	Work Resources	Work Evaluation

The Environment
  Social Expectations
  Institutional Goals
The Process
  Policies and Values
  Program Objectives
The Plans
  Mission
  Programs
  Resources
Implementation
  Recommendation
  Decision Making
  Action
	Organizing
	Staffing
	Communicating
	Budgeting
	Coordinating
	Providing Facilities
	Providing Support
	Supervising
	Reporting
		Income Development
		  Prices and Market
		  Governments
		  Philanthropy
		Allocation of Resources
		  Output Programs
		  Support Programs
		  Capital Programs
		Technology
		  Methods of Work
		Productivity
		  Utilization of
		  Resources
			Effectiveness
			  The Accomplishment
			  and Quality of
			  Outputs
			Efficiency
			  The Relationship of
			  Outputs to Costs
			Accountability
			  Justification of
			  Utility, Quality,
			  and Costs

sources, and (4) work evaluation. All four components must be given careful thought and appropriate action in the process of producing the desired outputs of the university enterprise.

Entire books have been written about the management of business enterprises and of government services. To compress the thought and experience of many persons over many years into a single chapter is an impossible endeavor. The most that can be attempted here is an outline. Such an outline is presented at the beginning of this chapter. I shall provide only the most general kind of elaboration in the discussion which follows.

Strangely enough, current writing about colleges and universities in the United States seldom refers to management organization or to management processes. There has been a great deal of discussion about governance and leadership, as if these problems or concerns took precedence over any problems or concerns of management. The problems of management have been largely ignored. Some efforts have been made for a good many years to improve university management, making use of the experience in business and government. My own judgment is that most of this effort has had only marginal impact, primarily because the production processes of a university are very different from the production processes of business enterprises and of government agencies. Considerable progress has been made in the so-called "business" operations of the university: in financial services, in administrative and logistical services, in plant management, and in auxiliary enterprises. But these programs are incidental to, or supportive of, the output programs of the university.

The fundamental management concerns of a university involve the management of instruction, research, public service, and educational justice. The first three of these outputs, and to some extent the fourth one as well, are outputs which can be produced only by faculty members. The most important managers in a university are the faculty members themselves. The management effectiveness and the management efficiency of a university are accomplished primarily by faculty members.

In my judgment it is errant nonsense in an academic community to postulate a dichotomy, a cleavage, between faculty members and "management." The managers of learning are faculty members; the managers of support programs are professional support personnel. Faculty members as managers of output programs and professional support personnel as managers of support programs have to learn how to live and work together, because the university can operate as a learning environment in no other way.

I would argue that the faculty claim to participation in university governance is legitimate simply because of the faculty role as managers of learning. Governance in all kinds of enterprises begins with the expertise or specialists with experience and know-how about productive processes and productive outputs. The governance mechanisms of a college or university cannot make careful and rational decisions about instruction, research, public service, educational justice, and constructive criticism in the absence of the practical experience of faculty members.

In the sections of this chapter which follow, I am concerned primarily with the management by faculty members individually, in departments, and in colleges of a university. Thus I am concerned primarily with the management of instructional programs, of research programs, and of public service programs. To be sure, the processes enumerated here can also be applied, with appropriate modifications, to the management of support programs. I am more interested in the management of output programs.

The processes of management as outlined here are "universals" in the sense that these ideas or concepts are to be found in many different kinds of enterprises. What is needed in the management of learning within a university is to understand that these concepts do have applicability to faculty production of instruction, research, and public service.

WORK PLANNING

No part of the management process is more important than planning. Planning in the simplest possible terms is preparation for work, is preparation to undertake a job task. The preparation may be detailed, methodical, time consuming. Or the preparation may be sketchy, slipshod, and hasty. For most kinds of undertakings man has found that the more careful the planning the more likely will the desired end product be accomplished within the limitations of work technology and work resources.

A degree program of instruction is a plan. A curriculum, or set of course offerings, is a plan. A course is a plan. A staffing pattern of faculty competencies or specializations within a department is a plan. A proposal for a research grant is a plan. A proposal for a public service project is a plan. A department budget is a plan. A college budget within a university is a plan.

For a university, planning begins with attention to the external environment. This external environment has various aspects: demographic, economic, social, and political. The number of youth of college age may fluctuate—there were substantial increases in the 1960s and substantial decreases in the decade of the 1980s. The state of the national and regional economy affects higher education enrollment in various ways: the labor market demand for educated talent in particular fields of specialization influences student enrollment; an expanding economy expands the demand for educated talent; a contracting economy lessens the demand for educated talent; the economy in recession tends to encourage enrollment because the opportunities for remunerative employment are less available; the economy in expansion tends to reduce enrollment because there is the alternative of available jobs; an expanding share of gross national product required for government services may restrict philanthropy and may lead to a public demand for reduced taxation. The social expectations for higher education involve the encouragement of social mobility, of social participation, of civic virtue, and of individual intellectual and cultural satisfaction. Government planning by means of the political process determines what kinds of higher education services to encourage or to contract, and the extent of the access to higher education services available to particular individuals. The external environment is a vital factor in university planning.

The university is more, however, than simply the product of external forces. The university may have some part in determining its own role. The scope of instructional programs, the research emphasis, the extent of public service endeavors, the quality of student admissions, the use of resources for student assistance, the effort to obtain income—all of these and similar concerns are the subject of extensive internal planning. Within some limitations—mostly economic for private universities and mostly governmental for public universities—universities may exercise some power in fixing their individual missions and their individual programs.

The process of planning within a university includes two somewhat different sets of concerns: (1) policies which evidence the basic commitments and value judgments of the university and (2) program objectives which evidence the specific work outputs to be accomplished. A university has a policy on the quality standards to be met by students entering an instructional program; a university has an admissions program which is intended to produce the desired quantity and quality of student inputs. A university has a policy on academic freedom; the personnel program ensures the observance of that policy. A university has a policy that public service projects must have specific external sources of income meeting both direct and indirect costs of operation; the program of public service projects exemplifies this policy position in operation. A university has a policy of emphasizing undergraduate instruction in general education and in the arts and sciences; the degree requirements and the instructional programs offered ensure the observance of this policy.

The basis of planning within a university is program planning. The programs of the university become the work planning units or centers of the university. Insofar as outputs are concerned, the work planning units are the various instructional programs, the various research programs, the various programs for creative activity, the various public service programs, and the various student financial assistance programs. Insofar as the support effort is concerned, the work planning units are the various programs of academic support, of student services, of plant operation, of institutional administration, of auxiliary enterprises, and of transfers.

In addition to program planning, a university must necessarily prepare various university-wide plans: an enrollment plan, an organizational plan, a personnel plan, a facilities and capital budget plan, a budget plan for current operations, a management information plan, and an evaluation plan. I shall return to this subject of program plans and of university-wide plans in the discussion of leadership.

As I have pointed out earlier, program plans set forth work objectives and workload to be accomplished by the organizational units of the university. The university-wide plans set forth the management policies and processes whereby program objectives are to be accomplished and evaluated by the university as an enterprise.

The end purpose of planning is the preparation of plans. A great deal of time in a university can be spent in studying demographic trends. A great deal of time can be spent debating the objectives and the program components for instruction in general education. A great deal of time can be spent arguing about organizational structure, about qualifications for tenure, about the allocation of resources for student financial assistance, about the reporting of student enrollment, and about the evaluation of teaching effectiveness. Study, discussion, and argument are phases of a planning process. At some point in time, however, planning is expected to result in plans, in a proposed course of action.

The plans of a university entail a statement of mission, a set of program objectives to be accomplished (output programs, support programs, university programs), and an analysis of resources (sources and utilization). Plans are proposals for action. Plans represent work outputs and work processes to be realized. Plans remain plans, remain proposals or recommendations for action, until decisions are made to carry them out.

The final stage in university planning is the stage of implementation: the recommendation of action to be taken, the decision whether or not to undertake the recommended action, and then the actual process of executing the decisions which have been made. The recommendation of action is a management task; a plan is the proposal of managers as accepted or modified by the leadership of the enterprise. The decision about plans is made by the governance structure and process of the university. We shall be examining this governance structure and process in the next chapter. The process of executing the decisions is once again a management process.

Planning in a university should of course be both long range and short range. It seems to me that universities as enterprises ought to look as far ahead as ten years; I doubt the utility of attempting any longer time span in seeking to anticipate future expectations and requirements. In contrast with long-range planning, intermediate planning might look five years ahead. Short-range planning is usually more specific, concerned with work objectives and resources one or two years beyond the current year. Planning needs to be short-range, intermediate, and long-range. I believe universities ought always to have at hand a five-year plan, and when the budget is adopted for the next year the five-year plan should move ahead another year.

Planning is necessarily closely tied to budgeting. I fail to see how the two processes can be performed except in close relationship one to the other. A budget is next year's work plan. A work plan is next year's budget. No constraint is so essential in planning as that of budget. No constraint is so essential in budgeting as that of work plans. The process of adjustment between work plans and work budgets never ends.

Necessarily, planning is a continuous process. Work experience and work evaluation result in modifications in work plans. Changes in the external environment may be frequent. Internal circumstances may alter university expectations; the sudden availability of a large endowment may well change mission and programs. The prospect of reduced support from governmental appropriations and grants means adjustment in programs. The planning process is as continuous as the operations of a university. To be sure, there is an alternative to planning. That choice is to react to circumstances and situations rather than to try to modify or control them. To some extent planning is always reactive. To some extent university plans are always tentative, subject to unexpected change in enrollment expectations, income projections, and economic crisis (such as a strike, a disruption in the delivery of energy, or a natural disaster such as flood or tornado). University planning can be incidental, based upon continuation of present circumstances, or university planning can be purposeful, envisaging adjustment to dramatic change in growth or contraction.

Needless to say, planning for the dramatic change of growth is quite different from planning for the dramatic change of contraction. Somehow, the university as an enterprise has found it simpler and more acceptable to adjust to the prospect of expansion than to adjust to the prospect of reduced scale. Small may be beautiful in the eyes of some economists and some humanists. But a decline in organizational health is troublesome and full of anxiety for all participants in the organization. When confronted with the reality of contraction, few universities, as aggregates of individuals, expect to be beautiful through being smaller.

WORK PERFORMANCE

Work performance means doing the planned job. Work performance means turning out the planned outputs. For the university, work performance means instructing students, undertaking a research project, engaging in creativity, accomplishing a public service, and promoting educational justice. In addition, work performance in a university means providing academic support (learning resources) for output programs, and delivering services to students. Work performance means operating and maintaining the physical plant, and providing other essential financial, logistical, administrative, and auxiliary services.

Work performance has long been understood to involve certain common processes. In *Papers on the Science of Administration*,* Luther Gulick created the acronym POSDCORB. The letters stood for planning, organizing, staffing, directing, coordinating, reporting, and budgeting. Gulick suggested that all of these processes were vital to the management of work in an organized enterprise.

The outline at the beginning of this chapter shows a similar set of words that identifies the processes of work performance. We could devote several lengthy paragraphs to an exposition of these terms and could examine their particular applicability to the enterprise of a university. With some brief elaboration, let me assert that work performance in a university does involve management processes long familiar in the literature of business and government enterprises.

The concept of organization has two somewhat different meanings in the context of the university, and I believe it does also in the context of other kinds of enterprises. In this essay I have been concerned to direct attention to the general structure for management, governance, and leadership. Beyond this, however, is another concern; namely, whether organization is for support management or for output management. A traditional structure of management organization in the university is outlined in Chapter 4. That outline, which need not be repeated here, is basically an organizational structure for both output and support management within a university.

---

*Luther H. Gulick and Lydall Urwick, eds. (Fairfield, NJ: Kelley, 1937).

Two or three propositions related to the university structure for work performance may be added here. The traditional pattern of organization involving academic departments, intermediate aggregations labeled colleges, and an enterprise aggregation called a university is not easy to change. Academic people are as set in their ways and as loathe to experiment with unfamiliar organizational arrangements as are any other group of people. We should note that organizational structure reflects work specialization and also program operations. It is easy to say that organizational structure should respond readily to changes in work specialization and program endeavors. It is not any easier in the academic community to bring about such organizational change than it is in any other enterprise.

For example, the work specializations that the university labels the arts and sciences (biological sciences, foreign languages, letters, mathematics, physical sciences, psychology, and social sciences) at the undergraduate level of instruction have three different program purposes. One program purpose is general education: stimulation of the student to understand the intellectual heritage of Western culture. A second program purpose is to provide the intellectual foundations upon which various professional specializations are built (such as the health professions, communications professions, information processing professions, education and counseling, law, and social welfare). A third purpose is to produce specialists in these various fields of intellectual endeavor. The academic departments representing these specializations have had considerable difficulty in organizing their work performance to provide separate identification and accomplishment of these different program objectives.

The importance of staffing, of personnel recruitment and retention, to work performance is obvious. It is customary to point out that the university is a labor-intensive enterprise, that its work technology and its resource utilization emphasize the personal services of faculty members and other categories of personnel. In accordance with varying circumstances, between two-thirds and three-fourths of a university current operating budget will be devoted to the compensation of individuals who comprise the staff of the enterprise. In large part the quality of a university is the quality of its staff.

The very essence of university instruction is the art of communication, of transmitting ideas and skills from one person to another. Communication is also the lifeblood of the university as an enterprise. Probably no organization ever achieves the effectiveness it aspires to accomplish in communication among the participants of the enterprise, among all the persons who are the personnel of the enterprise. But no complaint is more commonly heard on any university campus than the complaint that there is very poor communication within the organization. I could speculate at length about the reasons for this apparent failure; I am inclined to believe it is inherent in the very nature of the university. Faculty members believe that academic managers above the level of the academic department don't hear their expectations; and academic managers believe that faculty members don't hear the "facts of life" that constitute the environment of the academic community.

In an organization, communication as a vital process of work performance is the achievement of a shared understanding of a shared purpose. Faculty members, students, and staff share a common organizational setting, but appear never to achieve a shared understanding of a shared purpose. Communication among the work specializations of the university in the interest of achieving a common understanding of the desired work outputs appears to be especially complicated.

The subject of budgeting as an essential process of work performance will be noted in the next section of this chapter.

The process of coordination is a phase of work performance in the university which seldom obtains the acknowledgment it deserves. Beyond the level of the academic department, the levels of coordination are the college and the university. Within a university there is almost always some conflict about just how much coordination is needed at the college level and just how much is needed at the university level. Coordination never comes easily within a university. Academic departments are like aggregations of specialists wherever they may be found: they have a turf to defend. Each individual faculty member and each academic department believe that their activities are uniquely important and different from any other. Occasionally faculty members and departments enter into cooperative arrangements with other faculty members and departments, but these joint endeavors seldom work out over a considerable period of time.

Coordination as a process seeks two objectives: (1) to ensure that the work efforts of individuals and groups fit some general pattern and produce the desired output with minimum friction and without overlap and (2) to bring about some common standards (workloads, compensation, resources) among individuals and groups having comparable job assignments throughout the enterprise. Because there are so few agreements within a university about the competencies of an educated person, the coordination of instruction is difficult to achieve. Universities usually have been more successful in achieving coordination of their personnel and other university-wide plans.

Work performance requires facilities (buildings and equipment) and support services. Within universities a great deal of attention is given to these needs; the restrictive factor is of course the availability of resources to meet these needs. Faculty members and students tend to want a substantial array of support services: larger offices and laboratories, more secretarial and stenographic assistance, more teaching and laboratory assistance, more library books and periodicals, more instructional equipment and supplies, more travel funds, more student counseling, more extensive student health services, more recreational programs and facilities, more athletic programs and facilities, more student financial assistance, better food service, larger residential rooms, prompt payment of accounts, better telephone service, unlimited reproduction of various materials, more parking facilities. All these facilities and support services, at the department level and university-wide, are highly desirable, and highly expensive. The costs of support services are costs that must compete with faculty salaries, both in terms of numbers of faculty members and in terms of average compensation.

From the point of view of faculty members and students, the facilities and support services are almost never adequate for the desirable performance of the work outputs of instruction, research, public service, and educational justice. From the point of view of support program managers, their budgets are never adequate to respond to faculty and student expectations. From the point of view of university leaders and governing boards, a major priority is the number and compensation of faculty members and a second priority is the allocation of resources to facilities and support services.

Another aspect of work performance is supervision of the job efforts and outputs of the workforce. Because faculty members are professional practitioners of highly specialized educational preparation who over a period of time have acquired extensive professional experience, supervision of their professional performance requires careful and sensitive attention. In learning, as in other professions, there can be professional malpractice. Like other professionals, faculty members are reluctant to evaluate their fellow professional practitioners, to make a finding of professional malpractice, and to instigate corrective action (including expulsion from the profession).

Supervision really begins with the development of standards of professional performance and of professional ethics. Only in recent years have faculty members in some universities begun to formulate such standards. When standards have been prepared and officially adopted, then some supervisory authority must be assigned the responsibility of overseeing the observance of these standards and of instigating some appropriate action in instances of nonobservance.

Finally, in connection with work performance, the importance of adequate reporting deserves emphasis. Faculty members, and other managers in universities, frequently complain about the paperwork they have to complete. Reports are desired about enrollment, attendance (perhaps), and student performance. Other reports are desired about workload and the distribution of time among instruction, research, and public service. Time devoted to instruction may be divided among class hours, laboratory hours, preparation hours, student advising hours, and managerial hours (department and committee activities). Still other reports may be needed, such as those on student placement.

Reporting can be burdensome in any organization, including a university. Yet there is no substitute for reporting as the basis of a management information system and as the basis for an evaluation process. Reporting needs to be both statistical and evaluative, quantitative and qualitative. Reporting needs to be oriented to work performance and to organizational performance. Reporting is a foundation of communication, an opportunity and an obligation for a university to be informed about itself.

WORK RESOURCES

Colleges and universities obtain their income from three primary sources: charges or prices, government subsidies, and philanthropy. Table 4 shows the distribution of income for all public and private colleges and universities in the United States, according to the most recently available data.

In 1977, the total current income of colleges and universities as enterprises came to about $44 billion. Of this total

Table 4. Distribution of income for all public and private U.S. colleges (percentage).

	Public	Private
Charges		
Tuition and fees	13%	37%
Sales and services		
Educational activities	2	2
Hospitals	5	9
Auxiliary enterprises	11	13
Other income	3	8
Governments		
State	45	2
Federal	13	13
Local	5	1
Philanthropy		
Gifts	2	10
Endowment income	1	5
Total	100%	100%

SOURCE: National Center for Educational Statistics, *Financial Statistics of Institutions of Higher Education, Fiscal Year 1977* (Washington, D.C.: Government Printing Office, 1979).

income, $29.5 billion were received by public colleges and universities, and $14.3 billion were received by private colleges and universities.

For public colleges and universities, the income sources were distributed as follows:

Charges	34%
Governments	63
Philanthropy	3
Total	100%

For private colleges and universities the income sources were distributed as follows:

Charges	69%
Governments	16
Philanthropy	15
Total	100%

There were differences among colleges and universities by type (universities, other four-year institutions, and two-year institutions) and by location. Universities, public and private, received federal research grants while other institutions received very small support of this kind. Local government support was concentrated among two-year institutions. The residential college or university received substantial income from auxiliary enterprises, while the commuting college or university did not.

Nonetheless, the essential difference between the public and the private college or university is in the respective importance of charges and of government subsidies in providing the primary source of income. It is also notable that philanthropy provided 15 percent of the total income of private colleges and universities but only 3 percent of the income of public colleges and universities.

The role of governments in assisting higher education is not fully revealed by statistics of college and university income. In addition to grants for current operations, the federal government and almost all state governments provide some direct support to students to assist them in meeting the tuition and residence costs of college or university enrollment. It has been estimated that of about $9 billion spent by the federal government in support of instruction, research, public service, and student aid, about two-thirds was spent on student aid and was generally directed to students rather than to colleges and universities as such. Of college and university charges to students for tuition and room and board, as much as 25 percent may have been paid by students from income the student had received from government sources.

It has been said of colleges and universities generally that those who consume its product do not purchase it, that those who produce the product do not sell it, and that those who finance the product do not control it. To a considerable extent there is some truth in this observation. Students "consume" learning but pay only part of the cost of production. Faculty members produce learning but do not sell it. Governments and philanthropy subsidize learning but in general do not control that learning.

It is obvious that if colleges and universities are to expand their income, they must do so by increasing their prices to students and to clients, by persuading governments to enlarge their subsidies, or by soliciting greater support from philanthropy. It seems likely that the income development of the 1980s will have to give appropriate attention to all three endeavors.

While there has been some safety for colleges and universities in diversity of support, it is also evident that increased support may not be easy to obtain in the next decade. Charges to students and clients may discourage student enrollment and the consumption of educational services. Confronted by a "revolt" of taxpayers and harassed by demands for other services, governments may demonstrate a lesser interest in providing subsidies to higher education in the future. And the appeal for philanthropic assistance will have to depend upon sentiments of loyalty and upon an enlightened understanding of self-interest, which may or may not characterize alumni and friends in the next several years.

In the allocation of resources, colleges and universities distributed their income as shown in Table 5.

The distribution of available current resources for public and private colleges and universities was as follows:

Output programs	59%
Support programs	41%

Within these categories, however, the percentages were different for various programs. There were also considerable differences among institutions by type and by the residential or commuting characteristic of the student body. It will be noted that private colleges and universities spent a larger proportion of their available resources for student financial

Table 5. Distribution of income by colleges and universities (percentages).

	Public	Private
Output Programs		
Instruction	36%	27%
Research	8	9
Public service	5	7
Student aid	3	7
Hospitals	7	9
Support Programs		
Academic support	8	6
Student services	4	4
Plant operations	9	7
Institutional administration	8	10
Auxiliary enterprises	10	13
Transfers	2	1
Total	100%	100%

aid, a partial off-set to the higher proportion of income obtained from student tuition. Private colleges and universities tended to spend more for auxiliary enterprises, reflecting the residential character of so many of these institutions.

The practice of preparing and presenting comprehensive university budgets tends to conceal more than it reveals, and provides inadequate information for budget planning. A more useful but little utilized management process is that of preparing and analyzing component budgets. The comprehensive, university-wide budget is in fact a composite of various internal budgets. These internal budgets are especially important for management analysis.

In a university there are at least six major component budgets. If a university is involved in the operation of an "independent" research or public service facility for a federal or state government agency, then there may be a seventh component budget, one for independent operations. The usual six-component budgets for a university with a school of medicine are as follows:

Instruction.
Research.
Public service.
Hospitals.
Student aid.
Auxiliary enterprises.

These component budgets have in common two basic characteristics. Each component is a budget of *income* as well as of expense. Because so much income of a university is received for a particular program, or a restricted use, component budgets entail specialized income sources. Thus, in the budget for hospital operations a major source of income is payment by patients of hospital care charges, and perhaps of medical care charges as well. The student aid budget includes income from government, endowment, and gift sources earmarked exclusively for financial assistance to individual students. The auxiliary enterprise budget includes income from room rents, food service charges, bookstore sales, and other similar income. The research budget includes income from grants and gifts specifically designated for particular research projects or centers.

The essential factor in component budgeting is the relationship of funding sources and designated kinds of income to program expenditures. Just as universities have multiple outputs which they produce, so they have multiple sources of income, much of it for restricted use. Program expenditures require income, and component budgeting is a technique for planning and evaluating program costs in relationship to the income generated by those programs. The technique of component budgeting can also be applied to parts within the principal components outlined above: to a college of business administration, a college of law, or a college of medicine within the category of instruction; to a research project or a research center within the category of research; to student residence halls or student food service within the category of auxiliary enterprises.

An important consideration in component budgeting is the determination of the "fair share" of university overhead to be added to the direct costs of various programs. It is customary not to add overhead to the cost of student aid programs, although the management of student financial assistance is becoming an increasingly burdensome expense for universities. Sometimes only a part of the appropriate overhead cost is added to research expense, to public service expense, to hospital expense, and to auxiliary enterprise expense. When the overhead allocation to component budgets fails to add up to the total support costs of the university, the remainder is almost always included in the component budget of instruction. The fact is that overhead costs do have to be paid for from some source of income. If some component budgets pay less than their fair share of overhead, other component budgets must then pay more.

Capital budgets are just as important as current operating budgets. Capital budgets may be financed by special capital improvement appropriations, by gifts and grants, and by borrowing. When capital budgets are financed by borrowing, then the current operating budget must carry an expenditure category of "mandatory transfer." The transfer payment in this context is a setting aside of current income for debt service, like the payment of a mortgage on an individual dwelling.

The work resources of a university include a production technology. For the most part the management of a production technology rests with the individual faculty member. Learning usually occurs within the context of a course instructed by a single faculty member. The learning objectives of the course, the methods employed for learning, and the evaluation of learning accomplishment by students are determined by the individual instructor. There are various methods of instruction, from a lecture to a Socratic dialogue; there are various learning procedures, from textbooks and monographs to laboratories and field study; there are various aids to learning, from audiovisual materials to computers and television; there are various methods of evaluation, from examinations and standardized tests to written papers and demonstration of skill. All these work processes fall basically in the province of the management performance of a single faculty member in relation to one or more students.

The technology just sketched pertains to student instruction. Other technologies are involved in research, creative activity, and public service. The technology of research is the technology of advancing knowledge, the basic modes of procedure in undertaking scientific or other inquiry. These procedures may include the development of a formal theory, experimentation with mathematical models, laboratory or field inquiry, data collection, deductive logic, and the expression of new theory. These procedures may include clinical investigation, case studies, and statistical analysis. In creative activity there is a technology in writing, in artistic expression, in skilled performance. In public service there are many technologies available for the communication and demonstration of knowledge, experience, and skills. Again, in a university it is the scholar/researcher, the scholar/artist, and the scholar/practitioner who individually devise and perform the work technology needed to produce the desired outcomes.

Finally, this discussion of work resources must include work productivity. We have emphasized throughout this discussion the multiple outputs of university work effort. One of the complications in establishing standards for faculty work output and in measuring work accomplishment is simply the matter of deciding which work outputs to emphasize and to encourage.

Productivity in student instruction is customarily expressed in terms of a faculty/student ratio (1:4, 1:10, 1:20), in terms of student credit hours of enrollment (360 student credit hours, 240 student credit hours, 120 student credit hours), or in terms of courses taught per academic year of two semesters (5 courses, 6 courses, 8 courses). The student instruction productivity of a faculty member reflects the instructional technology appropriate to the content or to the level or to the quality of the instructional process; the proportion of a "full-time" faculty workload devoted to student instruction; and student enrollment demand.

There are other resources to be used in the instructional, research, creative activity, and public service processes besides faculty manpower. There are classroom and laboratory facilities to be utilized; there are learning resources to be utilized; there are residence and recreational resources to be utilized; there are support services (counseling, financial assistance, placement, and skill development) to be utilized. A university must be concerned with the productivity of all resources used.

A major issue for universities is the establishment and then the maintenance of standards of desired productivity. In turn, these standards depend upon income resources and upon student enrollment. If income declines or if student enrollment falls, resource use must be reduced or productivity standards will become lower and lower. Since the primary productive resource of a university is that of faculty members, an adjustment in numbers of faculty members or in compensation of faculty members becomes necessary when income declines and enrollment falls. Otherwise, productivity standards cannot be maintained, or costs cannot be contained. Because of concerns about the tenure status and employment security of faculty members, university management finds productivity adjustments difficult to achieve.

In this discussion of the management process of a university, we have made only incidental mention of students. It is essential to emphasize that learning does involve students as active, not passive, participants in the instruction process. And students (primarily graduate students) may be involved in the performance of research and public service. Students are a "work resource" of a university in several vital ways. Student learning is more than an output of a university; student learning is indispensable to the continuing endeavor of higher education. Student learning contributes to faculty learning and to faculty motivation. And student learning evidences the accomplishment of the university.

The management process of a university is concerned with students in several ways: the recruitment and admission of qualified students; the enrollment of desired numbers of students; the enrollment of the desired quality and skill of students; and financial assistance to students to encourage their enrollment and completion of a degree program. Management of a university entails student satisfaction as well as student learning.

WORK EVALUATION

Increasingly in recent years universities have been challenged to justify their existence, or more particularly to justify their claim to increased resources. As universities have sought to increase faculty compensation, to augment learning resources, to provide expanded services to students, to improve their support programs, and to cope with inflation (especially in energy costs), universities have had to obtain more income. As universities became interested in expanding their research, creative activity, and public service—or as they were asked to expand these activities—universities have needed more income. As universities were asked to enroll more students of diverse ethnic and socioeconomic status, they have needed more income for student financial assistance and for the development of student learning skills. As universities experienced increased enrollment demand in the 1950s to the 1970s, they have needed more income.

As the supply of educated talent produced by universities began to exceed labor market demand in the 1970s, and as research accomplishment within the universities appeared to be of little utility in meeting the emerging national problems of environmental pollution and energy resources and economic development, governments began to ask why educational outputs should rise in cost. Students began to ask whether or not learning was worth the cost of enrollment, including the loss of earnings they might have obtained in the labor market. Philanthropists began to ask why they should provide support to colleges and universities for high cost outputs of questionable economic value.

We cannot begin to try to answer these questions in detail, or to give them the attention they deserve. We must simply observe that as universities became more affluent and as their products cost more money, it was inevitable that these costs should come under question by students, by government officials and legislators, and by donors. As the outputs appeared to have a decreasing economic utility, it was inevitable that university costs should come under increasingly close scrutiny.

We may add here parenthetically that university leaders and university managers during the 1970s were often inept in responding to questions and criticism. On the one hand, they had little if any response to the criticism of "overeducating" Americans and, on the other hand, they had little if any response to the criticism that higher education was a waste of time and money for many students. Leaders and managers pleaded for income in the name of some "general benefit" produced by higher education without offering details about outcomes and costs.

In the changing environment of higher education in the 1980s, evaluation of work performance will become more and more important. All managers within an academic community will be expected to establish and maintain a continuing process of work evaluation.

Evaluation of a college or university is necessarily of two kinds: an evaluation of the people in an enterprise and an evaluation of the outcomes of the enterprise. Because the university is a labor-intensive enterprise, the performance of its personnel is of critical importance. If the quality of faculty, professional support personnel, support staff, and leadership within a university is superior, the performance of the enterprise will presumably also be superior. But the eventual evidence of quality performance by a university lies in the quality of the outputs produced: the quality of degree recipients, research, and public service produced.

Evaluation of personnel involves a what, a how, and a who. What shall be evaluated? How shall evaluation be undertaken? Who shall do the evaluating? The following is an outline of personnel evaluation:

What Faculty
        Instruction
        Research
        Public service
    Support personnel
    Leadership
How Performance objectives
    Performance measurement
    Cost/income analysis
    Corrective action
        Improvement
        Reassignment
        Termination
Who Student evaluation
    Departmental evaluation
    Peer evaluation
    Interdepartmental evaluation
    Accreditation evaluation
    Interinstitutional evaluation

A good deal of space would be required for a halfway adequate discussion of personnel evaluation. I would call attention simply to a few special concerns. Faculty evaluation involves three dimensions: instructional performance, research or creative activity performance, and public service performance. Faculty evaluation should be accompanied, in my judgment, by evaluation of the professional support personnel and of the leadership of the university as well. Evaluation must begin with a formulation of performance objectives. Performance measurement is a sensitive matter, because it can never be wholly objective. It is important, although not necessarily controlling, to know the cost/income relationship in personnel performance. Evaluation has little purpose if it does not lead to corrective action.

I could comment at length about student evaluation, departmental evaluation, peer evaluation, interdepartmental evaluation, accreditation evaluation, and interinstitutional evaluation. I will say only that all these arrangements have their strengths and their decided weaknesses. Personnel evaluation is never a simple process, and one reason is that people are always involved in the process of evaluating other people.

When it comes to evaluation of outcomes, the critical factors are effectiveness, efficiency, and accountability.

Effectiveness is the determination, or measurement, of work accomplishment in relation to work objectives. What did a particular output program or a particular support program undertaken in a given time period (one year or five years) intend to accomplish? How much of the intended output or the intended support was actually accomplished in that time period? In other words, effectiveness is the relationship of actual outcomes to planned outcomes.

The outcomes of a university have both a quantitative and a qualitative characteristic. The enumeration of quantities is simpler to undertake than is the assessment of quality, but both efforts entail substantial complexity for a university. It is relatively simple to count students, persistence in a degree program, and degrees awarded. It is relatively simple to inquire about the immediate status of a degree recipient: admission to further education, placement with an employer, nonparticipation in the labor market. It is far more complex to determine what students expected to accomplish through enrollment, why they dropped out, and how well their status upon completion of a degree program fitted their educational experience.

It is relatively simple to count research grants and projects undertaken; it is more complex to determine the knowledge advanced through research. It is relatively easy to count creative writing published, creative art works displayed, creative performances provided. It is more complex to determine creative achievement. It is relatively easy to count farmers consulting a county agent or visiting an agricultural demonstration; it is relatively easy to count the patients visiting a clinic or cared for in hospital beds; it is relatively easy to count enrollees in continuing education offerings; it is relatively easy to count requests for consultation or other assistance. It is far more complex to determine the benefits derived by individuals from all the various kinds of public service undertaken by the university. It is relatively easy to count the number of students obtaining financial assistance, obtaining assistance in skill development, or making use of other services. It is far more complex to determine whether or not such assistance and service enabled students to overcome economic and learning handicaps.

Regardless of complexity, managers of instruction, research, creative activity, public service, and student service need to give careful attention to enumerating and measuring work accomplishment in relation to work plans. University managers will be expected to know their work effectiveness and to respond to inquiries about that effectiveness.

The concern for efficiency is different from the concern with effectiveness. Efficiency is the measurement of costs in relation to output. Efficiency, moreover, is a measurement over time. The costs per unit of output this year or next year are compared with the costs last year or five years ago. Just as it is not too easy to determine the units of output to be enumerated by a university, it is not too easy to determine costs. Shall all direct faculty compensation and all faculty support costs be assigned to student instruction, or shall some of these direct costs be assigned to research, creative activity, and public service? How shall direct instructional costs be distributed by level of instruction: associate degree programs, baccalaureate programs, master's degree programs, doctoral degree programs? How shall overhead costs be allocated among degree programs, and among other output programs? These questions must be answered in order to determine costs per unit of output, such as a degree granted or a student credit hour instructed.

And over a period of time costs per unit of output may vary for many different reasons: the number of students enrolled, the changing composition of the faculty by rank, the changing levels of faculty compensation, the changing quality of students enrolled, the changing costs of university overhead. Even when comparisons of costs per unit of output are made in terms of dollars of constant purchasing power, using the higher-education price index, there are still these other troublesome changes to be taken into account.

Regardless of complexity, university leaders and managers may expect throughout the 1980s to receive questions and challenges about the efficiency of work performance. As enrollment declines and as economies of scale are less available, costs per unit of output may be expected to increase in terms of dollars of constant purchasing power. Some reduced costs per unit of output may be experienced in public service operations if the volume of these operations should expand in the 1980s. Research costs are likely to increase as equipment becomes more and more expensive, as techniques of discovery become more and more exacting, as problems to be investigated become more complicated. University managers will need to know their costs, their record of costs in relation to outputs, and reasons for their cost experience.

Finally, work evaluation includes a standard of accountability. The word "accountability" has had considerable currency in higher education discussions of recent years, and yet has remained a much misunderstood criterion of evaluation. Howard R. Bowen has written that the idea of accountability is quite simple: "It means that colleges and universities are responsible for conducting their affairs so that the outcomes are worth the cost." This definition is as useful as any which might be formulated.

Just as effectiveness is the relationship of actual outputs to planned outputs, and just as efficiency is the relationship of units of output to costs of inputs, so accountability is the relationship of outputs and costs to social utility. Let us grant that a university is effective in accomplishing its planned outputs; let us grant that a university is efficient in the use of resources to accomplish its actual outputs. The question still remains whether or not the outputs were socially useful.

Social benefit is at best a vague kind of standard to apply to any particular goods or services. There are certain basic ingredients to individual and social well-being which are commonly agreed to be necessary: food, shelter, clothing, health. Many of us would add elementary education, secondary education, and higher education. We would employ various arguments related to individual need and social welfare. We would assert that individuals of intellectual and creative competence should have the opportunity to develop their abilities to the fullest extent possible. We would assert that individuals have an inherent drive to know, that knowledge is better than ignorance, and that a commitment to rational behavior is better than the practice of unfettered emotional behavior. We would assert that a liberal democracy and a pluralistic society need individual leaders and others concerned to evidence civic virtue. We would argue that a technological society needs individuals of high professional competence in the service of all members of that society. In these assertions do we perceive the social benefit of higher education.

This vision of the higher education benefit to society may be as much an article of faith as it is a conclusion based upon empirical evidence. Those of us committed to the cause of higher education are convinced of our faith and of our conclusions. Yet we must also confront the continuing necessity in our society to demonstrate reasons for our faith, and facts upon which our conclusions are founded.

The factors in accountability, however, are more than just utility; they include quality and cost. Do our colleges and universities produce youth of professional competence and civic virtue? Do our colleges and universities produce research that advances knowledge, and encourage creative endeavor that is exciting and satisfying? Do our colleges and universities demonstrate the application of knowledge and creative endeavor that offers individual and social benefit. In a word, does higher education produce quality?

Given that colleges and universities do provide educated talent, knowledge, and creative activity to our society, is the cost of these outputs reasonable? Could the same outputs be produced for less cost? Would society be equally advantaged if we produced the same quality of outputs in a smaller supply at a smaller total cost?

In the 1980s, leaders and managers in higher education must have answers, convincing answers, to all these questions. The questions are reasonable. The answers will also have to be reasonable if they are to convince students, chief executives, legislators, benefactors, and friends.

Work evaluation has become an indispensable part of the management process in higher education.

CONCLUSION

To some people, these observations about the management process in the university will appear to be mechanistic rather than inspirational, to be concerned with means rather than with ends, to be oriented to bureaucratic behavior rather than to intellectual and creative behavior. To some extent, those critics will have reason for their expression of anxiety.

Great teaching may continue to be a high art. The ability to discover new knowledge and to synthesize knowledge may remain a rare talent. Creative competence may always be in short supply. Skilled performance in the use of knowledge to meet persistent problems may be unusual rather than usual among professional scholars. No amount of process can ever be a substitute for great teaching, for the discovery of knowledge, for the evidence of creative talent, for the demonstration of skilled professional performance.

The management process became important in and of itself within the university when we expanded greatly the scope of our products, the magnitude of our productive effort, and our expenditure of economic resources. When higher education became more affluent than ever before in its history, more indispensable than ever before to individual and social well-being, more sizable than ever before, then higher education became management oriented and was challenged to justify its resource use. Good management is the responsible management of resources provided in large part by social action. Concern for management is the price the university pays for its status in society and in the economy.

6

Governance
of the
University

Governance is the act of deciding what to do and how to do it within an organization. Within a university, governance involves decisions about the basic purpose or mission of the enterprise, about policies (values) to be observed and achieved in pursuit of the basic mission, about programs to be performed, and about resources to be obtained and utilized. Governance also involves decisions about enrollment objectives, organizational arrangements, personnel standards, facility requirements, information needs, budget allocations, and evaluation processes.

Although I insist that there is a clear distinction to be made between management and governance within a university, I recognize that there is also a close interrelationship between the two structures and processes. The literature and

GOVERNANCE OF THE UNIVERSITY

Laws and Regulations	The Governing Board	State and Federal Governments

University Ombudsman	President	University Council

Faculty
- Faculty Senate
- College Faculties
- College Committees
- Department Committees

Students
- Student Senate
- Student Residences
- Student Organizations
- Student Academic Units

Professional and Support Staff
- Staff Council
- Academic Support Staff
- Student Services Staff
- Technical, Clerical Trades, and Services Staffs

Alumni
- Alumni Association
- Alumni Board
- Alumni Chapters
- Alumni Staff

discussion about behavior in an organizational setting continually raise the question of a distinction between politics and administration, between policy and work performance. There are writers who insist that politics and administration in government cannot be separated; there are writers who insist that policy cannot be separated from work performance in business enterprises. There are others who argue strongly that politics can be separated from administration in government, and that policy can be separated from work performance in business.

The distinction between management and governance within a university is a part of this same effort to postulate different kinds of behavior, and different kinds of issues, within the academic community. I think it is possible to draw such a distinction, but it is never a simple matter to do so. More important, I think it is essential to the effective and efficient operation of a university to continually make the effort to draw this distinction. A failure to do so is to undermine the primary nature of the university as a productive enterprise, and to spend endless time debating details of operation when the need is for work performance.

I must repeat here the simplistic definitions I have used before. Management is work planning and work performance. Governance is decision making about purposes, policies, programs, and resources. This distinction is simplistic because it does not suggest the high degree of interrelationship between the two processes, nor the constant difficulty of determining just when a particular issue is to be considered an issue of management or an issue of governance. Let me cite an illustration of this complexity within a university. The enunciation or adoption of a policy of academic freedom for faculty members and for students is obviously an act of governance. The enactment of a standard of acceptable faculty and student conduct in campus protest is obviously an act of governance. The application of the standard to individual instances is an act of management, and the determination of a violation and of an appropriate penalty is an act of judicial decision. But faculty members and students often see in the act of management and in the act of judicial decision a change in policy or in standards of acceptable behavior within the academic community.

The complexity of management and of governance within a university arises from the unique roles of both faculty and of students within an academic community. As I have insisted earlier, the faculty member is not an "employee" of the university; the faculty member is a manager of learning. The student is not a "customer" of the university; the student is a participant in a formalized process of learning, and on a residential campus the student is a resident of the university. These roles, I would argue, necessarily involve both faculty members and students in university governance.

THE GOVERNING BOARD

The official and formal structure of governance in a university vests the legal authority and responsibility for decision making in a governing board of lay members who come from outside the academic community and who serve only part time. As a rule, members of a governing board serve without compensation; they contribute their services to the university as a matter of public obligation. In many instances members of governing boards receive no travel reimbursement for attendance at board meetings.

A mentor of mine once told me that a university president expected three attributes in a governing board member: wisdom, work, and wealth. The university desires to find all three characteristics in a board member; at a minimum, I was told, a university ought to find at least two of these attributes in its board members.

During the 1930s, and to some extent in the 1960s, the composition of governing board membership was attacked on the grounds that members tended to be white, Protestant, male, wealthy, older, and conservative. In the 1960s and 1970s many universities began to broaden the base of board membership to include blacks, Catholics, women, the less affluent, younger persons, and liberals. The ability of governing boards to provide wisdom, work, and wealth may have been sacrificed to some extent in the process of change, but some compensating advantages have been realized also.

There is not space here to consider the role, and the contribution, of governing boards in the detail the subject deserves. In 1975, on behalf of the Association of Governing Boards of Universities and Colleges, John W. Nason prepared a very helpful statement on the role of trustees, their major responsibilities, and the ingredients for effective service. Nason outlined ten major responsibilities of a governing board, as follows:

1. Selection, retention, and termination of appointment of a president.
2. Financial support and management.
3. Maintenance of the physical plant.
4. Public relations.
5. Clarification of institutional purpose.
6. Assessment of performance.
7. Provision of a bridge between campus and society.
8. Preservation of institutional independence.
9. Service as a court of final appeal in internal disputes.
10. Evaluation of board performance.

There is a complication in the governing board arrangement for many state universities and colleges because so many of them are part of a multi-campus system. For various historical and other reasons, the prevailing pattern of governance for state universities and colleges is the multi-campus system. The principal problem in this arrangement is the likelihood that the influence of lay governing board members will be separated from the learning process of an individual campus; this influence may then tend to become more politically oriented rather than learning oriented. Moreover, some multi-campus systems have tended to become quite bureaucratic in their handling of university problems, and to seek common solutions or uniformities of action rather than unique responses to the circumstances of a particular campus.

On the other hand, the multi-campus governing board may have certain advantages. It encourages older and established universities to assist in the creation of newer universities; this practice was especially important in the decade of growth during the 1960s. It promoted some diversity among universities. It realized some economies in support costs. And it broadened the geographical base of support in a state legislature for public higher education. In addition, state government officials often found it convenient to deal with multi-campus systems rather than with individual universities.

The role of governing boards is often misunderstood. From an early date in the history of American higher education, governing boards began to leave "academic" matters to the determination of presidents and faculties. These academic matters included degree requirements, the curriculum, instructional procedures, faculty personnel selection, admission standards, and even student conduct regulations. In public universities, because the faculty personnel process was outside civil service law and legislative determination, governing boards established faculty personnel policies and approved both appointments and salaries. For the most part, matters of appointment and salary received routine action by the board; on occasion, boards have intervened because public attention had been attracted to some faculty member or administrative officer.

Presumably, governing boards may delegate authority and responsibility for decision making on important matters to the president of the university, to a faculty senate, or even to a student senate. This delegation may be slated in university by-laws, or in a formal ordinance of governance. This delegation may be decisive or advisory. If faculty and student governance roles have tended to become more highly formalized in recent years, the authority of these roles has also tended to become increasingly advisory rather than decisive. Governing boards have found it necessary to become more heavily involved in many aspects of academic operations in recent years because of conflict within the academic community.

It is commonly said that the most important assignment of a governing board is the appointment of a president, and then afterwards the evaluation of presidential performance. This assignment is of course important. But I am inclined to believe that at least two other functions of the governing board are of equal importance: the approval of the university budget, and the role as a bridge between university and society. The final responsibility for the financial integrity and well-being of the university rests with the governing board. This responsibility cannot be delegated to a president or to any other body, in my judgment. In addition, the governing board is the agency that must constantly remind faculty members and students of the social support of the university, and of the social obligations that social support entails. The academic community cannot be self-governing when it is not financially self-supporting.

THE PRESIDENT'S ROLE IN GOVERNANCE

I shall say more about the president's role in relation to the governing board in Chapter 7. The president of the university is an agent of both the governing board and of the faculty. Students would insist that the president is their agent as well, although that claim is somewhat more difficult to substantiate. The president is the professional adviser to the governing board. The president is the enterprise-conscious adviser to the faculty and to the other constituent groups of the academic community. The president seeks to maintain a certain balance internally between the interests of faculty and of students, while fulfilling the obligations of budget execution. The president seeks to maintain a certain balance between the academic community and society. The president is almost always the person in the middle, and occupying a middle ground in any controversy is a sure prescription for attack from two sides.

THE FACULTY ROLE IN GOVERNANCE

I would argue that the faculty role as managers of instruction, research, creative activity, and public service necessitates a faculty role in governance. The difficulty arises in defining the faculty competence in governance, and in providing the appropriate structure for participation in the governance process. Colleges and universities wrestled with both aspects of the faculty role in governance during the 1960s and 1970s, and few colleges and universities would be willing to assert that they have found the satisfactory solution.

In writing about the governance of colleges and universities in 1960, John J. Corson * observed and articulated a concept of "organizational dualism." Although he did not identify the distinction in these particular terms, Corson in effect pointed to a fundamental difference between issues of academic and faculty affairs on the one hand and issues of

* *Governance of Colleges and Universities* (New York: McGraw-Hill, 1960).

"institutional affairs" on the other hand. In this second category Corson listed issues involving finance, student affairs, alumni and public relations, and physical plant. He pointed to two somewhat distinct processes within a college or university involving these two different kinds of decision making.

In 1962 * I argued that the academic community consisted of four principal constituent groups, which I then identified as faculty members, students, administrators, and alumni. I expressed the point of view that the decision-making process within the academic community was not so much one of organizational dualism as it was one of consensus building among these constituent groups.

In any event, I believe that after 1962 events on many campuses demonstrated that organizational dualism was no longer a viable concept or prescription for governance within a college or university. The student "revolution" beginning in 1964 presented in an acute form the question whether or not campus disturbance was an academic issue or an institutional issue; obviously the issue involved both faculty and institutional interests, not to mention student interests. Moreover, faculty members themselves insisted that they must be involved in budget and other institutional interests; the "new depression" of higher education after 1968 encouraged this insistence.

In revising his earlier work in a new book published in 1975, John J. Corson abandoned any mention of organizational dualism. Instead, he advanced two new concepts, one of primary authority and one of communal (or institutional) authority. He argued that the "primary authority" of the faculty should be reaffirmed to formulate policies and to take action on such "fundamental" concerns as curricula, the subject matter and methods of instruction, research, faculty

* *The Academic Community* (New York: McGraw-Hill, 1962).

status, and student academic performance. He argued that the "primary authority" of students should be clearly established to formulate policies on social and extracurricular activities. Finally, he argued that the obligation of the president to provide leadership for a college or university needs to be more generally recognized.

As I have studied and thought about the desirable governance structure within a university, I have returned to a concept of organizational dualism that does recognize a primary authority for the faculty in matters of academic and faculty affairs and that does provide for faculty participation in a consideration of institutional affairs. I think some university experimentation in combining the governance of academic affairs with institutional affairs has not been satisfactory, either from the point of view of faculty members or from the point of view of the institution.

Insofar as the faculty role in governance is concerned, this role should recognize the primary concern of faculty members in the management of learning and should provide a participative status for faculty in the consideration of university-wide matters of governance. Such a prescription affords faculty domination in formulating purposes, policies, programs, and budgets relating to instruction, research, and public service, while involving faculty members as one important group in formulating purposes, policies, programs, and budgets relating to the university as a whole.

In terms of structure, it is necessary again to distinguish between the faculty management structure and the university management structure. Faculty management of learning necessarily raises issues in the governance of a learning environment. Faculty members need to be heavily involved in the governance matters which affect the ability and the competence of faculty members to produce learning outcomes. And faculty members need to have an appropriate voice in the governance matters which affect the ability and the competence of a college or university to be an effective place of learning.

At the level of the individual faculty member and at the level of the academic department, the tasks of instruction, research, and public service are essentially managerial in nature. The tasks involve substantive matters of course objectives, course content, course instructional methods, course instructional resources, and the evaluation of student performance in a course. These tasks further involve issues of research projects and of public service projects, including time assignments, faculty availability, and income arrangements. A good deal of faculty time is likely to be devoted to faculty personnel matters, including faculty recruitment, faculty promotion, faculty tenure, faculty compensation, and faculty development. All of these academic and faculty issues are likely to raise issues of governance, to raise issues involving changes in purposes, policies, programs, and budgets.

At the department level it may not make much sense to undertake a distinction between management problems and governance issues. To some extent, the department may be able to resolve its management problems internally; in general, governance issues may require action at the college level or even at the university level. The department executive officer may formally or informally solicit and consider the advice of department colleagues. One arrangement for such consultation in a large department may be an executive committee of senior members or of elected members of the department. The executive officer is well advised to resolve problems and to raise issues in conjunction with the assistance of other members of the department.

I had the pleasure of being the member of an academic department with an executive officer who gave a great deal of his time to consulting with his colleagues. All members of the department met on a monthly basis to review matters of concern. In addition, the executive officer conferred almost on a daily basis with his principal colleagues to keep them informed of the department's problems as he saw them. The practice of consultation by this executive officer was injurious to his own scholarly accomplishment, but it was conducive to the development of a strong and harmonious department.

The department executive officer is more, however, than a chief manager. He or she is the representative of the department in the management and governance structure of the university. In a university (as distinct from a college), the next level of management and a primary level of governance is the component college, presided over by a dean. While the college issues are concerns both of management and of governance, the principal problems are likely to be issues of governance: degree requirements, the allocation of resources among departments, the appropriate actions to maintain the strength and to overcome the weaknesses of particular departments, the quality of student recruitment, the quantity of student enrollment, desirable changes in program objective and program scope, and standards of personnel and program performance. The executive officer of a department becomes in effect a managerial associate of the dean in formulating policy recommendations on all of these and related subjects.

At the college level, I have suggested earlier that in their managerial roles college deans need at least two faculty committees to assist them: a planning committee and a personnel advisory committee. On matters of governance—degree requirements, program offerings, admission standards, personnel standards, budget needs—a college faculty is likely to wish to act as a whole. College faculties may meet as often as monthly in some situations; other faculties may wish to meet quarterly or even once a semester.

It seems to me that in addition to faculty meetings the dean of an academic college needs an executive committee to review governance issues and to present recommendations to the faculty. In my judgment, this executive committee ought to include the department executive officer and one elected faculty member from each department. The executive committee might appoint ad hoc committees to study particular problems and to present proposals to it. Faculties tend to have too many committees and to waste a good deal of valuable faculty time in committee meetings. The fewer the committees, the more time faculty members can devote to the pressing problems of instruction, research, creative activity, and public service.

I believe strongly that the dean of an academic college should serve as presiding officer of a college faculty and as chairman of the faculty executive committee. There is some question whether or not college faculty decisions should be conclusive. On budget matters, college faculty participation can only be advisory. On degree requirements and program offerings, the college faculty decision may be final, or it may be only a recommendation to the university-wide faculty. This question must be resolved campus by campus.

Finally, there is the faculty role in governance at the university-wide level. On academic and faculty affairs at the university-wide level, I believe there should be a faculty senate presided over by the vice-president for academic affairs. When there is a health science center as part of a university, a separate faculty senate for health affairs is desirable. In large universities (with enrollments of over 6,000 students) a faculty senate of academic deans and elected faculty representatives from each college seems to me to be the preferable governance structure.

It is not unusual for a university-wide faculty to wish to preserve some matters for their vote. I know of one instance in which the faculty constitution required that a vote of "no confidence" in the president could only be taken in a university-wide faculty session. Nearly 3,000 faculty members were present for such a vote. I know of another instance in which a university-wide faculty vote was required in order to adopt a recommendation for the award of an honorary degree. In another instance, any matter receiving a majority but not a two-thirds vote in the faculty senate required a vote of the university-wide faculty.

A university-wide faculty meeting is obviously a kind of town meeting. In a university of 10,000 students there will be 500 or more persons with faculty rank. In a university of 30,000 students there will probably be 2,000 persons with faculty rank. An assemblage that large can scarcely become a deliberative body, but the idea of all faculty members having an equal voice in university governance may require periodic meetings of the university-wide faculty.

A faculty executive committee may be desirable in addition to a faculty senate to serve as a screening device for agenda items and to authorize ad hoc committees from time to time to study particular issues. Moreover, I believe strongly that the vice-president for academic affairs should preside over the executive committee and over the faculty senate, and that academic deans should participate in both bodies. Faculty members properly insist upon a voice in the selection of academic deans and of academic vice-presidents. Having participated in their selection, faculty members can scarcely assert that these officers are not part of the academic establishment of the university.

I would emphasize that the scope of concern for a university-wide faculty senate extends to academic affairs and to faculty affairs. Moreover, at the university-wide level the actions of a faculty senate must be considered as advisory to the governing board. It is a desirable arrangement to resolve as many academic matters and faculty matters as possible at the college level. If an academic policy or program or a matter of faculty policy or standards requires university-wide attention, then that policy, program, or standard would seem to me to require governing board approval as a final action.

There remain two other items to mention. I shall say more about faculty participation in a university council later in this chapter. I believe such participation is essential; as important as a faculty senate is, a university council is also important and requires faculty membership. The faculty senate is needed to consider academic and faculty questions; the university council is needed to consider university or institutional questions.

The other item is that of faculty membership on the governing board. I agree with the position of the Carnegie Commission on Higher Education taken in the Commission's 1973 report on governance. The Commission declared that faculty members should not serve on governing boards but might well serve on appropriate board committees. I would add that faculty members through a chapter of the American Association of University Professors (AAUP) or through other channels ought to have the privilege of presenting their point of view on any governance issue directly to a governing board.

Faculty membership on a governing board is undesirable for two basic reasons. First, the governing board is supposed to represent the reaction of laymen, not the reaction of professionals, to the learning concerns of the university. This lay reaction should obviously be well informed, but it should remain a lay reaction, or at least the reaction of persons not having a personal interest to protect. Second, faculty membership on a governing board might encourage increased board attention to various academic and faculty matters better resolved below the level of the board.

Faculty governance within a university is a difficult structure to develop and to operate. It seems to me that the experience of the 1960s and 1970s, an experience I have undertaken to analyze elsewhere, suggests that there is a dual set of somewhat distinct if not interrelated matters to be resolved within a university. A primary authority of the faculty in matters of academic and faculty affairs should be recognized. But faculty involvement in university affairs is also needed. The preferable governance structure, I think, is one which accommodates both kinds of governance needs.

THE STUDENT ROLE IN GOVERNANCE

As I noted earlier, the student of a university is a participant in the learning process. On a residential campus, the student is a citizen of the academic community. In both these roles the student has a major interest in the learning requirements and the behavior standards expected by the university.

The serious issues of student participation in governance which arose in the 1960s and 1970s in the United States primarily concerned the privileges and responsibilities of the student as a citizen of the academic community. The issues involved privileges of protest (which unfortunately in some instances degenerated into violence) on public and social matters: the war in Vietnam, racial discrimination, poverty, and environmental pollution. The issues involved privileges of protest on student conduct regulations: standards of student behavior, standards of membership in student organizations, the establishment of residence halls housing men and women together, visitation hours for men and women in residence halls, student services to be provided on campus, the cost and allocation of special charges or taxes for students.

Only to a limited extent did student protest involve academic and faculty affairs: degree requirements (especially required courses), standards of admission and academic performance, the tenure of popular faculty members, the evaluation of faculty performance from a student perspective. On occasion, the issues of protest might involve issues of university-wide governance: relationships with a surrounding urban community, services to the poor and to minorities, the investment of endowment funds in corporations doing business in Rhodesia and South Africa.

The response of universities to the protests of students was to endeavor to structure a formal role for students in the governance of the university. The adoption of the 26th Amendment to the Federal Constitution in 1971 giving the right to vote to all citizens who are 18 years of age or older encouraged state governments to lower their age of majority to 18 years, and promoted a popular conception that persons at 18 years were to be considered as adults. Student participation in university governance was a recognition of student adulthood.

In general, student participation in university governance took two forms: (1) increased delegation of authority to student government, and (2) student representation in a university council or other similar body. Student government in one form or another had existed on most college and university campuses since World War I. This student government was not very influential, to be sure, but it did exist. Student representation in a university council was something new.

In the 1960s and 1970s faculty bodies increasingly divested themselves of the authority to enact student conduct regulations. This authority was turned over to a student affairs council or to a university council, often with final authority of approval remaining in the hands of the governing board. Student affairs entailed not just a code of student rights and responsibilities but also the scope and financing of student services and standards of membership for student organizations.

In some instances, university by-laws specified a certain rate of participation in student elections if student government was to be considered a legitimate voice of student interests and concerns. Such a desired or proper rate of participation might be fixed at 30 or 40 percent of all registered students. As the 1970s proceeded, student concern with student government seemed to be receding on many campuses. Perhaps the issues of concern were considered to be largely resolved.

One problem of student government structure was that of

the basis of representation. Should it be by academic units (arts and sciences, business, engineering, fine arts, and so on), by year of degree status (freshman, sophomore, junior, senior, graduate), by residence (dormitory, off-campus, commuter), by organizations (fraternities, sororities, honorary societies, publications, student associations), or by a combination of such representation? It seemed evident that representation by living units was especially important on a largely residential campus, particularly on issues involving dormitory life.

Another problem was that of student participation in academic and faculty affairs. Faculty members often were disposed to believe that students did not have a proper role to perform in the resolution of issues involving academic and faculty matters. Faculty members expressed the attitude that students lacked the experience and perspective to judge the intellectual and professional concerns of faculty members. On the other hand, students (and undergraduate students in particular) expressed the attitude that student interests were frequently ignored or given slight attention by faculty members.

Some student involvement in academic and faculty affairs would seem desirable on a campus. It might be useful for the dean of a college to have a student advisory committee made up of senior students at the undergraduate level, and perhaps a separate graduate student advisory committee. Department executive officers might also find a student advisory committee useful, especially executive officers of large departments. These student committees might meet quarterly or three times a year, and might be invited to express opinions on any academic or faculty matter of concern to any individual student. Some mechanism of communication at the college and the department level seems appropriate to the status of the student in the learning process.

In a number of university settings, especially in public universities, students in the late 1970s were becoming increasingly concerned about charges to students. Some of this attention centered on the student fee or "tax" in support of student services, student activities, and student organizations. The position was sometimes asserted that a student "tax" should be appropriated only by student government. This position ignored the fact that the authority to tax students was vested only in the governing board, which also had responsibility for final approval of appropriations from the tax. To be sure, this governing authority could be superseded by authority of the state legislature. In addition, students wanted stable or reduced tuition. Faculty members, academic leaders, and governing boards wanted increased income, some of which had to come from increased prices to students.

During the 1970s in several states student governments on state university campuses began to form a state-wide association of students as a means of representing student interests before the state legislature. This effort meant that students had to begin to learn the refinements of influential lobbying in a state capital. In some instances the lesson was well learned. The complication was that student interests and university interests might well be in conflict. University leaders therefore had an additional good reason to involve students in the governance structure and process on campus.

On many campuses, a major objective of student activism has been membership on the governing board. Some states have by state law provided for one or two students to serve on a governing board, and in other instances private colleges and universities have provided for one or two students to be included on the board of trustees. In still other instances, charters or by-laws have been amended to provide that one or two board members shall be a recent graduate of the college or university.

The Carnegie Commission on Higher Education recommended that students should not serve on the governing board of the university where they are enrolled. The Commission did advocate student membership on appropriate committees of a governing board, and the privilege of direct presentation of student concerns to a governing board. I would agree with these positions. In their enthusiasm as young adults, students often appear to assert that there is something especially moral and proper about their particular interests. Students often seem to believe that all interests other than their own are especially immoral, irrational, and obstinate. A major defect in student attitudes is an insistence upon freedom from social responsibility while being dependent upon social economic support.

If students are not as well informed as may be desirable about the problems of the university they attend, the fault may well lie with the faculty and the leadership of the university. If students do not understand that university positions on behavioral standards, political protest, and endowment investment may affect university income, including income for student financial assistance, students may not have been provided adequate financial information about the university. If students do not understand that decisions about programs, services, access, standards of quality, and financial assistance require increased income from governments and from philanthropy if student charges are not to be increased, then their education about higher education may have been neglected.

The objective of student participation in university governance is the development of responsible citizenship within the academic community on the part of students. It is an objective worthy of commitment and continuous endeavor.

THE STAFF ROLE IN GOVERNANCE

Apart from faculty members, there has been a disposition on the part of many university leaders to ignore the proper claim of other staff members for participation in governance. On a residential campus in particular, the number of persons involved in the support staff may exceed the number of faculty members. In any event, the support staff is too important a group to leave outside any structure and process of internal governance.

Apart from faculty members and the executive leadership group of a university—this group will be further identified in Chapter 7—the support staff of a university includes a wide variety of positions. In the standard classification of personnel for a university, only two categories would be excluded from staff status: faculty members and students. The categories of staff personnel would be the following:

Administrators and managers
Specialists and support professionals
Technical employees
Office and clerical workers
Craftsmen and tradesmen
Service employees

One of the complexities for participation of these groups in an internal governance structure has been the diversity in positions held. Both the administrative/managerial category and the specialist/professional category tend to identify themselves and their interests with the executive category of personnel. The other categories of personnel have little in common insofar as type of work performed is concerned; they do have in common a concern with prevailing rates of compensation and with general working conditions within the university.

It would appear to be desirable to organize a staff council with representatives from each of the categories of personnel listed above, with membership roughly proportionate to the full-time strength of each staff category. It would be desirable for such a staff council to meet two or three times a year simply as a communications arrangement.

Where I have had occasion to observe a staff council in action, I have always found it difficult to identify common interests among the participants. This situation has been especially evident when most staff members are included in a state civil service system and have their compensation and their hours of work governed by state civil service law and regulations. Under these circumstances, staff members have sometimes found it useful to belong to an association of state civil service employees as a means of presenting their interests for consideration by the state legislature.

An alternative to a state civil service association for many staff members has been collective bargaining. The American Federation of State, County, and Municipal Employees has been active on many state university campuses in seeking to organize technical, clerical, crafts, and service personnel and in representing this staff through collective bargaining. At private colleges and universities, various union organizations have sought to organize the same categories of staff and to represent this staff in collective bargaining.

Unionization seems to be a likely response of support personnel if these staff members perceive themselves as being paid less than the prevailing compensation of the area, and if these staff members perceive themselves as being generally neglected in the structure and process of internal governance.

THE ALUMNI ROLE IN GOVERNANCE

Finally, the alumni body of a college or university should be considered as a major constituent group of internal governance. At best, alumni are likely to be an amorphous group of persons engaged in many different kinds of professions and having many diverse interests. Some alumni will evidence a sense of appreciation and obligation for their higher education experience, while others will look back with very little regard for the college or university where they pursued a degree program.

Colleges and universities seek to identify and enlist the interest of those alumni who maintain some continuing loyalty. This loyalty may be expressed by annual or other financial giving, by assistance in student recruitment, and by participation in various alumni meetings (local and national). Occasionally, alumni of a state university may be mobilized as a political interest group, but this kind of effort is likely to be sporadic rather than continuous.

The customary arrangement is for a college or university to organize a national alumni association, and to arrange at least two annual meetings of alumni on the campus. Usually one other meeting a year will be held in major urban areas where a sizable number of alumni may reside. Both kinds of occasions are used to provide information about the current status of the university: its problems and its prospects. In addition, the various alumni publications afford an additional means of communication.

A national association of alumni will usually elect a board of directors, a certain proportion of the directors being elected annually for terms of from three to seven years. In turn, the board may annually elect a president of the alumni association. Alumni voting is generally done by mail ballot and the voting is restricted to those who contribute a nominal amount (5 or 10 dollars) each year to the alumni loyalty fund. This alumni board may meet two or three times a year to review various aspects of the alumni program and to make suggestions about modifications or additions to alumni endeavors.

The governance problem is that of determining the organizational relationship of the alumni association to the university. Basically two models have evolved. One is the model of separate incorporation as a nonprofit educational corporation or foundation formed to advance the work of a particular college or university. The other model is that of an organic relationship in which the alumni association is considered to be a constituent part of the higher education corporation and the director of the alumni program is considered to be an administrative officer of the university. For obvious reasons, university presidents tend to favor the second model but on occasion have found it necessary "to get along with" the first arrangement.

In either structure, the president and his or her staff associates need to give particular attention to the alumni association. They need to consult closely with the alumni board members, to keep in touch with alumni concerns, and to inform alumni of the needs and problems of the university. To the extent that an alumni board and an alumni association perceive themselves as having a voice in university affairs, they can be looked to for support, financial and otherwise.

UNIVERSITY COUNCIL

The discussion up to this point has been concerned primarily with four constituent groups of an academic community: faculty, students, professional and support staff, and alumni. Each group is likely to be different from the others, to have different interests and concerns, to voice different attitudes about the university, to offer somewhat different ideas about the mission and the programs of the university. None of these groups can be ignored by the president, by the president's executive associates, and by the governing board.

Organizationally, it appears desirable for the president formally to associate all four of these constituent groups with the decision-making process through the device of a university council. It is preferable for this council to have an advisory role to the president rather than to the governing board simply because the advice is needed during the formulation of recommendations on basic issues to be made by the president to the governing board.

There are several organizational difficulties in defining the composition and the scope of interest on the part of a university council. Insofar as scope of interest is concerned, it seems advisable for a president to consult with and seek the advice of a university council on all the non-routine matters to be presented to the governing board for action. The desirable composition of a university council may be somewhat more difficult to determine.

Faculty members are likely to insist that they ought to have a majority, or at least a plurality, of the membership. They are likely to oppose membership by a president's executive associates on the grounds that these individuals are simply an extension of the president's personality. Faculty members are also likely to oppose extensive membership on the part of students or of alumni, on the grounds that these groups have too little understanding of the intricacies of instruction, research, creative activity, and public service.

This faculty point of view might be given greater weight than it otherwise deserves if the agenda of a governing board was predominantly concerned with academic and faculty affairs. While instruction, research, creative activity, and public service are indeed the end purpose of a university—along with educational justice and academic freedom—the issues which are likely to occupy, or should occupy, governing board attention are issues about how the university can facilitate the accomplishment of these ends, not how the faculty can or should realize these ends. And on the general subject of facilitating the accomplishment of basic purposes, faculty members may have no greater expertise than students, staff, or alumni. Faculty members are likely to have even less expertise on the university as a learning environment than the president and the president's executive associates.

The objective in university governance should not be to

encourage governing board attention to academic and faculty affairs. On the contrary, the objective should be to resolve as many as possible of all academic and faculty problems through internal management and governance processes. Only those academic and faculty affairs with repercussions of a public interest—admission standards, the thrust of academic programs, the general qualifications of faculty personnel, the resources available for academic programs, the general standards of faculty behavior, the quality of expected student performance—only such academic and faculty affairs should be brought to the attention of the governing board. To be sure, some faculty affairs must necessarily be approved by the governing board of a state university; these affairs include faculty personnel actions and faculty compensation. But it is desirable that these matters be handled essentially as a routine of governance within the context of basic personnel and budgetary policy.

In a university council of 100 members, I have known the membership distribution to be 40 faculty members, 40 student members, and 20 administrative, staff, and alumni representatives. Apart from the concern that 100 members may indeed be too large for a consultative body, the proportional distribution may be appropriate. The student membership is then coequal with the faculty membership, and both together substantially outnumber the administrative, staff, and alumni membership. Internally, such a relationship may be desirable, especially if we may assume that the executive leadership voice and the alumni voice will be clearly heard by the governing board in any event.

Some question has been raised on various campuses about the presiding officer of the university council. I do not understand how the university council can expect to be a useful mechanism in internal governance unless the president is the presiding officer. It is the president whom the university council is expected to advise. It is the president who is expected to provide professional leadership to the governing board. It is the president who is expected to have the major role in making certain that governing board decisions are implemented in action. Under these expectations, the president should have the opportunity to discuss his or her concerns, and the university council should have the advantage of hearing directly the public interest concerns of the president. These advantages are best assured of realization when the president serves as presiding officer of the university council.

GRIEVANCE PROCEDURES AND DISCIPLINARY ACTION

The discussion of governance herein has emphasized the "legislative" function: the determination of policies, programs, rules of procedure and of behavior, and the allocation of resources. There is an additional function which needs to be accommodated within a university, and which is an appropriate subject for governance determination. This function is that of grievance procedure and of "judicial" process.

In an academic community, as in other organizational settings, there are inevitably individuals who believe that they personally have not been treated properly under established rules and practices of the university. Students may have academic grievances about degree requirements, evaluation of course performance, and rules governing academic conduct. Faculty members may have grievances about course assignments, support assistance, rank, compensation, tenure status, and retrenchment or retirement practices. Professional and other staff may have grievances about job classifications, workload, supervision, compensation, fringe benefits, and lay-off practices.

The adjustment of individual faculty grievances is an important phase of faculty personnel management, a continuing concern for department executive officers, academic deans, and vice-presidents for academic affairs. The adjustment of individual student academic grievances is an important phase of a faculty member's professional practice, reinforced by department and college committees or subcommittees authorized by faculty rules to make exceptions to academic rules and otherwise to adjust student complaints. The adjustment of professional and other staff grievances is an important phase of personnel management within the support services of the university.

During the general campus disputes of the 1960s and 1970s, many universities established the position of university ombudsman as a central complaint office and as a mediator of conflict between individuals and the organizational practices of the university. The office of ombudsman usually had no authority to settle any grievances, but the office endeavored to assist individuals in obtaining some appropriate review of their situation. Reporting to the university president as the officer usually did, the ombudsman was in a position to call attention to problem areas or problem managers within the university and to influence managerial or governance action to reduce or eliminate troublesome situations.

The absence of an effective grievance procedure has been one argument used in advocating faculty collective bargaining, or staff collective bargaining. A university is well advised through its governance process to establish some procedure for the consideration and adjustment of individual grievances.

Beyond the matter of faculty, staff, and student grievances, there is the further concern of enforcement procedure for the rules governing faculty, staff, and student individual behavior. Some universities with a sizable residential campus have had to establish traffic and parking regulations, and to enforce these regulations with a traffic court. Most univer-

sities have a set of rules governing faculty rights and responsibilities, staff rights and responsibilities, and student rights
and responsibilities. The judicial problem is one of determining whether or not an individual did violate one or more of
these rules, and of deciding the appropriate penalty to invoke
upon a finding of violation.

The customary arrangement in many universities is to
have one enforcement arrangement for faculty members, a
different enforcement arrangement for staff members, and a
third enforcement arrangement for students. The appropriate
enforcement arrangement in each instance is a matter of university governance, a matter to be determined finally by action of the governing board. The enforcement of faculty rules
is usually delegated in the first instance to a faculty judicial
board; the enforcement of staff rules is usually delegated to a
university judicial board; and the enforcement of student
rules is usually delegated to a student judicial board.

On occasion, university rules may authorize the president
to review the decisions of a judicial board and to reduce the
penalty if there is some reason to do so. A president needs to
be careful about the extent to which he or she can or should
be involved in such review. On a large campus a good deal of
time may be consumed in this kind of activity, and there is
always the danger of undermining the authority of a judicial
board.

In cases involving sensitive issues of considerable public
concern—cases such as those involving campus disruption,
faculty malpractice, student publications, and student organizational activity—the governing board may wish to become a court of last resort within the university. Here again
there are dangers of extensive time commitments and of
second-guessing internal judicial action.

In recent years the volume of individual grievances and of
appeals from "administrative action" taken to courts of law
has been on the increase. Courts of law have shown some

disposition to review university rules and their application to individual circumstances. Although legal appeal is likely to be expensive for both litigants, the individual and the university, the possibility of such an appeal is an incentive for careful university rule-making, and for careful university observance of the rudiments of due process in all quasi-judicial actions.

CONCLUSION

The governance of a university is a complex structure and process. The complexity is inherent in the very nature of instruction, research, creative activity, and public service as the learning outputs of the university as a productive enterprise. The governance structure and process necessarily reflect the unique requirements of organizational purpose.

The university comprises various constituent groups. Insofar as faculty members and students are concerned, the objective of the governance structure and process is to provide substantial autonomy in decision making. The limitations upon this autonomy arise from the unique economic aspects of learning, in which faculty members do not charge for what they produce and students do not pay in full for the benefits obtained. Neither faculty members nor students can afford to be indifferent to the external environment of the university.

Faculty, students, and staff within a university have been portrayed as engaged in an extensive political conflict with each other, and even within each group. No doubt there are differences in the interests of these groups as groups, and these interests are in conflict in various ways. A major conflict is the different economic interests of each group. The politics of conflict, to the extent that such conflict exists, must be resolved by the governing board. The resolution may seek a certain balance or compromise of these interests. The process of balance is advanced by the structural arrangement of a university council, if this arrangement exists and if it functions with some degree of utility.

At the same time, much of the potential conflict between the internal constituencies of the university—apart from conflict about the allocation of economic resources—can be contained by careful self-restraint on the part of faculty, students, and staff. The price of autonomy in internal governance for these various constituent groups is self-control. No organizational structure can impose limitations which are certain of observance. But the governance process can encourage conflict or it can mute such conflict. Which situation prevails will depend in part upon faculty, student, and staff attitudes. In part, the situation will depend upon university leadership.

LEADERSHIP OF THE UNIVERSITY

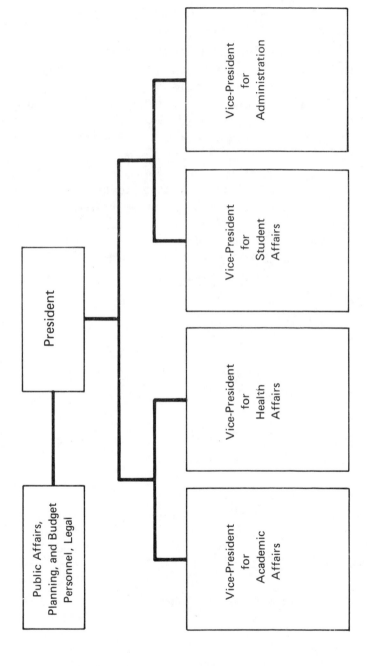

7

Leadership of the University

Leadership has long been a subject of fascination to historians and to students of social behavior. Are leaders born or are they produced by circumstances? Why do some critical times produce outstanding leaders and other critical times produce few if any leaders? What are the personal attributes of leaders? How do leaders become leaders? These questions are only a few of the many issues which scholars and others have pondered from time to time.

James MacGregor Burns* asserts that one of the "most universal cravings of our time" is a hunger for outstanding leadership. He goes on to say: "The crisis of leadership today is the mediocrity or irresponsibility of the men and women in power ... The fundamental crisis underlying mediocrity is

---

* *Leadership* (New York: Harper & Row, 1978).

intellectual." Burns insists that Americans as a people know too little about leadership. He postulates two kinds of leadership: *transactional* leadership and *transforming* leadership. He then acknowledges his special concern with moral leadership.

Most of us are aware that leadership has two attributes, personal and institutional. The personal attributes of leadership may include intelligence, courage, integrity, strength, physical presence, determination, perseverance, hard work, cunning, and even ruthlessness. The institutional attributes of leadership may include status, wealth, position, competent associates, special opportunities, a certain correlation between the expectations or aspirations of people and the performance of leadership.

In a democracy—indeed in any society—the purpose of leadership has long been argued. Burns distinguishes purposes with his use of the words transactional as opposed to transforming leadership. Is leadership the special ability or intuition of an individual to sense the drive or hope of a group and then to show the way to realization of that goal? Or is leadership the special ability or intuition of an individual to tell a group what it ought to desire and then to show the way to realization of that goal? Perhaps there are elements of both kinds of ability or intuition in most leadership situations.

Moreover, it is clear that different times and different circumstances may demand a different combination of leadership attributes. Conditions of crisis may require a transforming kind of leadership. Conditions of stability may require a transactional kind of leadership. Conditions of growth may require a transactional kind of leadership. Conditions of decline may require a transforming kind of leadership.

Our concern in this discussion is with leadership in the context of a particular kind of community, the academic community, and in the context of a particular kind of productive enterprise, the enterprise producing learning. In this kind of setting there are necessarily certain attributes expected of leadership: familiarity with and respect for the academic community and learning intelligence, emotional stability, managerial competence, the ability to motivate individuals to strive to advance their learning achievement. But we are particularly concerned here with some of the institutional requirements of leadership in the academic enterprise.

The leadership role of a university centers in the position of president. Recruiting and selecting a president is a major responsibility of a governing board, a search process in which governing boards do well to associate representatives of the faculty, the student body, and alumni. John W. Nason, in a report for the Association of Governing Boards of Universities and Colleges (1979), has suggested nine steps in presidential search, as follows:

1. Establishing the machinery of search and selection.
2. Organizing the committee.
3. Formulating the criteria.
4. Developing a pool of candidates.
5. Screening candidates.
6. Interviewing candidates.
7. Selecting top candidates.
8. Appointing the president.
9. Winding down.

This outline cannot begin to convey the wealth of practical advice, guidelines, and cautions contained in this very helpful little book.

Personally, I believe that no part of the selection process is more important than determining what characteristics of experience, age, ability, and interests the university seeks in a president at a particular time. Moreover, what a university needs in the way of primary emphasis at one particular time may be quite different from what a university needs at some other time. A university may have neglected its external con-

ı

stituencies and need a president to cultivate these relationships. A university may have neglected change in its institutional programs and need a president to stimulate a rethinking of educational purposes and program objectives. The two different kinds of need may well call for different characteristics of presidential leadership.

From time to time, selection committees and other groups have sought to establish the objectives of presidential leadership. Here is my own formulation of these objectives.

Understanding of and Commitment to
the Academic Community

1. The president demonstrates an understanding of faculty authority and responsibility in the transmission and encouragement of learning.
2. The president demonstrates an understanding of the role of scholarship and of creative competence in the advancement of knowledge and in the achievement of cultural expression.
3. The president demonstrates an understanding of public service endeavor as a means for demonstrating the utility of knowledge and the aesthetic appreciation of creative art.
4. The president demonstrates a commitment to educational justice in access to learning and to institutional services, as well as in institutional employment.
5. The president demonstrates a commitment to the responsible exercise of academic freedom.

Planning and Management Competence

6. The president is able to articulate an educational philosophy that is appropriate to the mission and circumstances of the institution.
7. The president exercises leadership in the development of academic policies and programs which implement the mission of the institution.
8. The president has the ability to organize a planning process involving all management units of the enterprise, to establish planning assumptions and parameters, and to formulate planning objectives for appropriate decision making.

9. The president has the ability to link both a current operating budget and a capital improvement budget with planning objectives.
10. The president has the ability to set forth program priorities and resource allocation consistent with available income.
11. The president has the ability to analyze organizational needs to deliver the output objectives of the enterprise and to provide the essential overhead (or support) programs of the enterprise.
12. The president has the ability to select highly qualified and acceptable individuals as leadership and management associates of the enterprise.
13. The president evidences a capacity to achieve sound fiscal management and the effective as well as efficient utilization of resources.
14. The president encourages and directs a continuing process of program and personnel evaluation.

Planning and Governance Competence

15. The president demonstrates an awareness of the internal constituencies of the academic community and involves them effectively in the planning and decision-making process.
16. The president demonstrates an awareness of the particular interests of the various internal constituencies and seeks to promote an appropriate balance among these interests.
17. The president demonstrates a capacity to formulate academic policies and programs which respond reasonably to the aspirations of faculty, students, and staff.
18. The president demonstrates an awareness of the external constituencies of the academic community and seeks their advice about desirable policies and programs without compromising the integrity of the institution.
19. The president demonstrates an awareness of the particular interests of the various external constituencies and seeks to communicate to them an understanding of academic values.
20. The president demonstrates a capacity to formulate academic policies and programs which respond reasonably to the expectations of external constituencies.
21. The president demonstrates a capacity to formulate and present recommendations to the governing board which have involved consideration of internal aspirations and of external expectations.

22. The president demonstrates the ability to mobilize external constituencies in the social, political, and financial support of the institution.

Leadership Style

23. The president demonstrates the capacity to articulate major problems confronting the academic community.
24. The president demonstrates the ability to analyze issues, to comprehend the multiple factors involved in major problem areas, and to consider alternative sources of advice about the appropriate resolution of problems.
25. The president demonstrates a capacity for flexibility in the face of opposition, and a willingness to reassess a position in the light of additional facts or further consideration.
26. The president delegates authority to associates and accepts responsibility for decisions and actions.
27. The president makes decisions on a timely basis, on a reasonable basis, on a fair basis, and accepts the consequences.
28. The president evidences a commitment to academic excellence and to moral principle.

If governing boards are to institute a periodic evaluation of presidential performance, that assessment must begin with a set of performance objectives. Evaluation is a useful, indeed legitimate, procedure only when the objectives of performance have been determined against which to measure actual accomplishment. The criteria for determining whether or not behavioral standards have in fact been realized are not very exact. In many instances, judgments must be made upon the basis of a limited number of facts or impressions. But the judgments are at least partially informed when they are made against a known set of standards.

LEADERSHIP AND AMBIGUITY

In a study undertaken for the Carnegie Commission on Higher Education and published in 1974, Michael D. Cohen and

James G. March * described the American college president as exercising a role of ambiguous leadership. Cohen and March asserted that the major features of the college presidency needed to be understood in the context of the peculiar characteristics of the American university as an organization. They asserted that the university belonged to a class of organizations which they labeled "organized anarchies." The general properties of organized anarchy were identified as: (1) problematic goals, (2) unclear technology, and (3) fluid participation.

Cohen and March declared that the American university did not know what it was doing. They argued that the organization seemed to operate on a variety of ill-defined preferences, and that it discovered these preferences through action rather than through planned endeavor. They asserted that the university could best be described as a loose collection of changing ideas rather than as a coherent structure of purpose.

Second, Cohen and March insisted that the technology of the enterprise was familiar but not understood. The university was described as operating on the basis of a simple set of trial-and-error procedures, on the basis of experience learned from accidents of the past rather than on the basis of designs certain to produce learning.

And in the third place, Cohen and March observed that the "major participants wander in and out of the organization." Faculty members and students varied in the amount of time they devoted to the effort of the organization, with the result that the boundaries of the organization appeared to be uncertain and changing. Cohen and March suggested that these properties were not limited to educational institutions but that they were especially evident in the university. At the same time, they failed to identify any other enterprises which they would classify as organized anarchies.

* *Leadership and Ambiguity* (New York: McGraw-Hill, 1974).

Because the president of a university was asked to provide leadership in an organizational setting of organized anarchy, that leadership role was ambiguous. How can leadership be effective when the goals are unknown? How can leadership be effective when the technology is unclear? How can leadership be effective when participation in the enterprise is fluid? Cohen and March concluded: "When goals and technology are hazy and participation is fluid, many of the axioms and standard procedures of management collapse." In a final chapter the two authors endeavored to suggest that leadership in an organized anarchy might be enhanced through certain "rules": spend time on major issues, persist, exchange status for substance, facilitate participation of opposition, undertake various projects, manage unobtrusively, and interpret history with some flexibility.

We might argue at some length whether or not Cohen and March have accurately portrayed the reality of the learning process within a university, and whether or not they have observed the leadership role of the president in its proper perspective. Indeed, I believe that they have misunderstood the leadership status of the university president. The president cannot lead faculty members in the design of course objectives, in the determination of course content and technology, and in the evaluation of student learning. The president cannot formulate a research project or guide faculty members in conducting a research project. The president cannot demonstrate tested skill in the application of specialized knowledge to a particular problem. In other words, a president cannot manage learning. Only faculty members can manage learning.

The goals of the higher learning are not uncertain. What remains uncertain are issues of priority, and of appropriate method. The instructional goals are the individual development of intellectual abilities or of creative talent, the preparation of persons for para-professional and professional careers, and the cultivation in individuals of civic virtue. There is disagreement among faculty members about the order of priority to accord these goals, and there is uncertainty among faculty members about how to achieve these goals. And then there are the additional goals involving the conduct of research, the sponsorship of creative talent, the performance of public service, and the promotion of educational justice. We repeat that there are few arguments within universities about these goals as goals. There is endless debate about the operational definition of these goals and about their order of social importance. And universities never have the income or other resources to produce the outputs they aspire to accomplish, or the outputs they consider socially beneficial.

The leadership of a university then must be exercised within the context of an enterprise dependent upon individual faculty members to produce the desired outputs with a technology faculty members individually devise but with resources they do not control. If this kind of leadership must be labeled ambiguous, so be it. I think it must be considered to be leadership within a unique kind of organizational structure.

DIMENSIONS OF THE PRESIDENTIAL ROLE

There is an external and an internal dimension to the role of presidential leadership in a university. The external role is primarily representational. The internal role is one of leadership of the academic community as a productive enterprise. Both roles are demanding and time consuming. Occasionally universities have experimented with their leadership structure and have designated one individual to be "Mr. Outside" and another person to be "Mr. Inside." The fact is that the two roles are interrelated, and are difficult if not impossible to fulfill in separation one from the other.

The representational role of the president involves the many "publics" of higher education. For a state university which is part of a multi-campus system, presidential representation begins with the governing board. Presidential representation includes relationships with the adjacent urban community, with a state board of higher education, with the state chief executive (and staff), with the state legislature (and staff), with federal government officials (administrative, executive, legislative), with alumni, with media of mass communication, with professions, with business enterprises, with general purpose foundations, with various associations, with church bodies, and with various "friends." This representation may be formal or informal; it may be handled personally, or by leadership colleagues, or by association executives.

The message of university representation is simple in theme, complex in detail. That message is one of individual and social benefit derived from the multiple outputs of the university. The implication of the message is always that the individual and social benefits could be multiplied if the resources of the university were multiplied. The demonstration of these benefits in specific and readily understandable terms is the continuing challenge of university leadership.

Another part of the message is an appeal to permit faculty members and students "to do their thing" with a minimum of external interference and control. On the one hand, the president pleads for increased resources; on the other hand, the president pleads for institutional autonomy. To many persons comprising the "publics" of higher education, the two pleas are inconsistent. If increased resources are to be provided the university, may not the donor of those resources expect some assurances that the claimed benefits are actually being accomplished, that the intended outputs from augmented income are in fact performed? There is a continuing tension externally between the search for funds and the imposition of controls. Presidential leadership of the university must cope with this tension. The internal dimension of presidential leadership involves guidance of the enterprise as an enterprise. If the president cannot manage learning, he or she must manage the organization as a learning environment. Management entails more than a balancing of expenditures with income, vital as this balancing is. Management entails effective and efficient use of available resources to the fullest practicable extent.

Just as faculty and student participation in the internal governance process is desirable, even basic, to decision making about learning purposes, learning programs, and learning policies, so in turn presidential leadership is essential as a continuing reminder of the social expectations from the enterprise and of the external sources of support. Perhaps a president cannot "demand" certain decisions or behavioral characteristics on the part of faculty or students, but a president can point to the external consequences of those decisions or of particular behavior. Decisions and actions within the academic community engender certain external perceptions of that community, and external perceptions affect external support. If faculty members are content to have lesser compensation, if students are content to pay more of the cost of their learning, then external perceptions and external support may be given slight attention. The academic community confronts choices, and presidential leadership involves clarifying both choices and consequences.

THE PROBLEMS OF PRESIDENTIAL LEADERSHIP

The discussions about planning in much of the higher education literature fail to make an important distinction between program planning and institutional planning. Making use of the program classification employed earlier in this discussion, we may identify the principal program categories involved in university operations as follows:

Output Programs
   Instruction
   Research
   Public service
   Student aid
   Hospital operations
   Independent operations
Support Programs
   Academic support
   Student services
   Plant operation
   Institutional administration
   Auxiliary enterprises
   Transfers

Planning for these programs is an integral part of the management of these programs, and is performed by program managers and program supervisors throughout the organizational structure of the university. Top management attention to these programs is distributed among the management associates of the president, as we shall note below.

Program planning, however, is only a part of the planning process for a university. A second part of that planning process involves what I shall label, for lack of a better designation, "university-wide" planning. University-wide planning is peculiarly the province of the university president.

University-wide planning includes the following component parts:

1. A statement of mission.
2. An enrollment plan.
3. An organizational plan.
4. A personnel plan.

5. A facilities and capital budget plan.
6. A current operations budget plan.
7. A management information plan.
8. An evaluation plan.

The task of internal leadership for the president of a university is to ensure that a planning process will produce university-wide plans, that university-wide plans lead to university-wide decisions, that information about the evaluation of planned performance does take place, and that planning and decision making occur on a continuing basis. As a leader of the university, the president is planner-in-chief for university-wide plans.

To be sure, program planning and university-wide planning are interrelated. Program plans must be prepared in the context of university-wide plans. University-wide plans must seek to fulfill the work objectives of program plans. Neither kind of planning within the university can proceed without careful attention to the other.

As an illustration of this interrelationship, let us look briefly at the preparation of an enrollment plan. Each academic department of a university has an implicit or explicit enrollment plan. Each aggregation of departments—a college of arts and sciences, a college of business administration, a college of education, a college of engineering, a college of fine arts, a college of medicine, etc.—has an enrollment plan. But the university enrollment plan is much more than a composite of component enrollment plans. It is a bringing together, reconciliation, and modification of component enrollment plans in terms of demographic trends, university mission, student interests, and university resources.

The ingredients of an enrollment plan are many. Externally, enrollment is influenced by such factors as the number of youth of the traditional college age, the participation rate in higher education of college-age youth, the labor market demand for educated talent, the service area of the university, the university's potential student enrollment, the inclination of older persons to enroll in degree programs, the cost of instruction to students, and the attractiveness to students of instructional program offerings.

Internally, enrollment is influenced by student interest in particular programs and faculty members, faculty interest in students, the standards required in student performance, student perseverance to a degree (or attrition from year to year), the experience in student placement, and general satisfaction or dissatisfaction with the learning environment.

Two major factors in enrollment planning are the qualitative standards of student access to various universities (and to various instructional programs within a particular university), and the availability of student financial assistance. Qualitative standards limit access to universities and programs; at the same time, the perception of university or program quality on the part of students may influence some students to increase their interest in seeking enrollment and influence other students not to seek enrollment. As a general proposition, the more resources a university has or spends for student financial assistance, the larger will be the enrollment. Programs seeking student enrollment will ordinarily seek increased funds for student aid. Oftentimes, the use of student financial assistance can determine student enrollment.

The whole subject of enrollment planning is critical to university operations because of its relationship to university financing. An increasing enrollment usually means more income; a declining enrollment means a declining income. The correlation is similar for both public and private universities. If the instructional output of a university is reduced, then resources may be shifted to other outputs, such as research and public service. If resources are not available to produce other outputs, then increased income must be obtained from nonstudent sources or resource use must be curtailed in order to balance costs with income.

Each of the subjects listed above as essential parts of university-wide planning could be considered here in some detail. The point of emphasis is simply that there is a need for university-wide planning in addition to program planning, that university-wide planning is indispensable to university operations, and that university-wide planning is peculiarly the task of presidential leadership. There is no substitute for university-wide planning, and there is no substitute for presidential leadership in university-wide planning.

COLLECTIVE LEADERSHIP

A well-known report * on administrative management in the federal government published in 1937 included a succinct and arresting statement: "The President needs help." From this beginning came the "institutionalization" of the American presidency as it functions today.

The same kind of statement may be made about the presidency in a university, or in any large-scale enterprise. The president needs help. The job of the university president cannot be performed by a single individual, except in a very small college indeed. The scope and size of the president's leadership staff will depend upon the enrollment and budget size of the university, and upon the scope of program activities. University leadership has necessarily become team leadership, or collective leadership.

The president of a university has need for two kinds of assistance. For lack of any better designation, I shall designate these as executive assistance and managerial assistance.

---

* *Administrative Management in the Federal Government*, prepared by the President's Committee on Administrative Management (Washington, D.C.: Government Printing Office, 1937).

It follows that there is a need for two kinds of assistants, executive assistants and managerial associates.

I shall refer to the managerial associates first, simply because these officers have been mentioned earlier and because attention to their respective tasks can be appropriately brief here. The managerial associates are the president's link to university management, to program planning and program performance. The managerial associates are the chief "managers" of the various university programs listed above and discussed in an earlier chapter. The managerial associates distribute among themselves the authority and the responsibility for the day-to-day work and the program planning of the university.

The managerial associates of the president usually include a vice-president for academic affairs, a vice-president for health affairs (if there is a medical college in the university), a vice-president for student affairs, and a vice-president for administration. We have indicated earlier how the program operations of the university are distributed among these managerial associates.

I would emphasize in particular that each of these managerial associates is both a chief manager of programs and a leadership associate of the president. If one believes, as I do, that a major part of the planning endeavor of a university, or of any enterprise, arises in connection with the operation of work programs, then each of these managerial associates has a primary role to play in the leadership as well as in the management of the university. Moreover, I employ the word "associate" in this relationship in order to emphasize the importance of each officer in undergirding the leadership role of the president.

Presidential leadership in a university depends in large part upon the competence, the loyalty, and the energy of these managerial associates.

The executive assistants to the president are of necessity

an extension of the personality and the role of the president as a university leader. The executive assistants do not manage program operations in the same sense as the managerial associates. We do on occasion speak of the "fund-raising program" of the university, but this "program" is different in that its objectives relate to the university as a whole, as an organized enterprise in its entirety. The executive assistants help the president to perform the work of the university presidency.

I find it useful to list the executive functions of the president in these categories:

Public affairs.
Planning and budgeting.
Personnel.
Legal.

Public affairs includes community relationships, government relationships, alumni relations, development, and public information. In a special way I would add to this listing the work of the admissions officer in representing the university to high school counselors, to the parents of prospective students, and to prospective students themselves.

A president may decide to organize all public affairs activities under a single individual, such as an executive assistant for public affairs or a vice president for public affairs. Or, a president may decide to have two or three specialists reporting separately to him or her in the public affairs area, such as an executive assistant for alumni relations and development, an executive assistant for government relations, and an executive assistant for public information. The organizational arrangement should fit the leadership style of the president and should accommodate the personalities involved. The important concern is that the scope and magnitude of the public affairs task should be recognized and should be given full attention.

An executive assistant for planning and budget is the organizational arrangement enabling the president to fulfill his role as planner-in-chief and budget officer of the university. Planning and budget may include a program planning office, a facilities and capital budget office, a budget office, and an office of institutional research (which might better be designated a management information office).

I believe strongly that program planning should be linked with program budgeting—in fact, the two really cannot be separated. Program planning fixes work objectives; program budgeting fixes the work resources to be utilized in the accomplishment of work objectives. Program planning without program budgeting is unrealistic. Program budgeting without program planning is meaningless. Both program planning and program budgeting must be brought together for the university as a whole by the university president.

I am well aware that many university presidents have found it convenient for reasons of past practice or for reasons of personal competence to make the vice-president for administration the budget officer of the university. This organizational assignment tends to recognize the affinity between budgeting and accounting, and since accounting is a task assigned to the vice-president for administration, there appear to be advantages in making this managerial associate the budget officer of the university.

While budgeting is necessarily closely related to accounting, I think the two tasks are sufficiently different to justify their separation. As I have just observed, program budgeting needs to be closely allied to program planning. Apart from considerations of personality and of personal relationships, I have another objection to the assignment of the budget task to the vice-president for administration, or to any other managerial associate for that matter (such as the vice-president for academic affairs). To be sure, all managerial associates are involved in program planning and program budgeting.

Each one is a separate and important claimant to the income resources of the university. To ask the vice-president for administration to serve as budget officer is to place that official in an awkward relationship with the other managerial associates. But even more troublesome can be the tendency of the vice-president for administration to set an example for his or her managerial colleagues and to practice foolhardy economies.

I have known vice-presidents for administration, for example, who, as budget officers of the university, have failed to press their proper claim for an adequate plant maintenance budget within the university. There are few universities in America that, during the 1970s, did not defer important expenditures for plant maintenance. As a consequence, many universities have consumed their plant capital and will enter the financially troubled decade of the 1980s with sizable needs in deferred plant maintenance.

Moreover, in the power structure of a university the vice-president for administration is likely to be in a poor position to press for reallocation of resources among the academic programs subject to the supervision of the vice-president for academic affairs. Faculty members often are inclined to consider the vice-president for administration as "the enemy," as one who doesn't understand faculty needs and faculty concerns. Sometimes presidents may find it useful to avoid the impression that the president is the enemy. In reality, the enemy, if there is one, is likely to be the internal aspiration of faculty members to do more than university resources can support. Presidential leadership is essentially seeking a balance between aspirations and income reality.

If a president desires the vice-president for administration to serve as budget officer, then it would be helpful if it were understood that one individual is in fact fulfilling two roles: the managerial role of vice-president for administration and the executive role of assistant to the president for budget. I believe the preferable organizational arrangement is to establish the separate position of executive assistant to the president for planning and budget.

I believe it is also desirable for a president to have an executive assistant for personnel. Affirmative action requirements of the federal government usually specify that there must be an affirmative action officer reporting directly to the president. What these requirements ought to specify is that there should be a personnel officer reporting directly to the president who is also incidentally, or in connection with his or her personnel duties, the affirmative action officer.

The standard classification structure for manpower resources in a university is as follows:

Instruction/research/public service professionals.
Executive/administrative/managerial professionals.
Specialist/support professionals.
Technical personnel.
Office/clerical personnel.
Crafts and trades personnel.
Service personnel.
Students.

This kind of classification structure may have to be modified somewhat within state universities to fit the requirements of state civil service laws, but as a general and meaningful outline of a personnel plan, the structure is quite useful. Under most state civil service laws faculty personnel and "principal administrative officers" are exempt from the classified civil service system.

Most universities operate three distinct personnel systems: a faculty personnel system (supervised by the vice-president for academic affairs), an administrative personnel system (supervised by the president or vice-president for administration), and a nonacademic personnel system. We are not concerned here with the details of any of these systems.

What appears to be essential today, for various reasons, is a comprehensive personnel plan which encompasses all three systems, relates a personnel position plan to the program plan and budget plan, and establishes standards for personnel management regulations on affirmative action, occupational health and safety, pensions, collective bargaining, and other personnel actions. Personnel planning and personnel management are more complicated and more exacting than ever before in a university. The president is necessarily the chief personnel officer of the university, and the president needs assistance in fulfilling this role.

Finally, in this enumeration of executive concerns we need to note the immense importance of legal affairs today. If the president does not obtain legal advice through a general counsel or legal adviser on a continuing basis, then the president must have legal assistance on a periodic basis as the need occurs. It is scarcely necessary to remark that universities are today involved in a wide range of legal disputes or legal requirements. Universities with increasing frequency are sued by faculty members and other personnel charging discrimination based upon sex, race, religion, or national origin. Universities are involved in disputes about contracts, in disputes about collective bargaining, in disputes about "fair consumer practices," in disputes about the publication of misleading information. Universities may be accused of violating environmental protection regulations, of enforcing unfair or unreasonable restrictions upon staff and student behavior, of failing to provide access and service to the handicapped. This legal litany might be greatly extended. The president of a university has to have help on legal matters.

It is customary in many universities for the president to bring together his or her leadership colleagues in a formal arrangement termed the "president's cabinet." The arrangement is useful in providing a forum for the discussion of leadership problems, for considering alternatives of desirable action, for anticipating future situations. I would emphasize two aspects about a president's cabinet. First, it is vital that such a cabinet should include in its membership both the managerial associates of the president and the executive assistants of the president. The two groups need to interact in the process of providing advice and assistance to the president. Second, it is vital to make a distinction in discussion between management issues (including the planning process) and governance issues. Governance issues must be resolved or decided eventually by a governing board. Governance issues should be considered by the university council in addition to the president's cabinet.

The president's leadership role is critical to the well-being of the university. The president is the link between management and governance, between the internal "world" of learning and the external "world" of social expectation and social support. The management of learning is the province of faculty members. The management of the university as an organized enterprise, as an environment of learning, is the province of the president. The university needs both if it is to achieve its high purpose in American society.

CONCLUSION

The language of this discussion will alienate many faculty members. The language of economic enterprise, the language of organization and management, the language of program planning and program budgeting, the language of governance and of power structures will seem exceedingly inappropriate to the art of teaching, the expectations of research, the excitement of creative activity, the benefits of public service, the pursuit of educational justice, the commitment to academic freedom.

Economics, management, and power are concepts alien to the faculty member's usual preparation as a scholar/teacher, as a scholar/researcher, as a scholar/artist. The faculty profession tends to be a profession of individualists. Even when exhorted to indulge in faculty collective bargaining as a protection against the fears and anxieties aroused by managers, governing boards, governors, and legislators, faculty members retain their innate disposition to be different one from another.

The organized anarchy observed by Cohen and March was not so much the organized anarchy of the university as it was the organized anarchy of the faculty profession within the university.

Personally, I have great sympathy with the faculty abhorrence of economics, bureaucracy, organization, and social constraint. At the same time, I have great sympathy with the faculty attitude that faculty members are generally misunderstood, unappreciated, and underpaid. When universities aspired to become especially important to American society and to be supported accordingly; when universities expanded substantially the instruction of students, the conduct of research, the sponsorship of creative activity, and the performance of public service; when universities became the stage for social protest in the 1960s; when universities became the hub of a knowledge society—then universities became the center of social attention and the center of economic concern.

With social attention and with economic concern came not just the language of economic enterprise and of organizational arrangements, but demands for explanation and justification.

This essay has endeavored to provide some degree of common sense about the management, governance, and leadership of the university. This essay has endeavored to present the university as a unique organizational device, unique because it serves in a particularly useful way a pluralistic society, an affluent economy, and a liberal democracy. And, if the fates be friendly, the university in America will continue that unique service for decades, even centuries, still to come.

Index